Wrongful Dismissal

WRONGFUL DISMISSAL
A Practical Guide

Julian Yew

The Law Society

Appendix 1 is Crown copyright and is reproduced with kind permission of Her Majesty's Stationery Office and the Department of Trade and Industry.

ISBN 1–85328–762–8

Published in 2001 by The Law Society
113 Chancery Lane, London WC2A 1PL

Typeset by J&L Composition Ltd, Filey, North Yorkshire
Printed by Antony Rowe Ltd, Chippenham, Wilts

'Hard cases make bad law. Bad cases make hard law'

per Lord Justice Sedley

Cerberus Software Ltd *v* Rowley *[2001]*

IRLR 160, CA.

Contents

CONTENTS

Foreword

A recent television advertisement which I found annoying but memorable had the punchline: 'it does exactly what it says on the tin'. This book is exactly what it says on the cover, a practical guide: key points of guidance are highlighted throughout the text; there are useful links to internet sites; the appendices contain helpful precedents and other information that one can so often spend valuable time trying to track down. It is a truly practical self-contained guide to bringing or defending a wrongful dismissal claim.

In a complex field, the layout and the clarity of the writing have addressed the issues involved in such claims, from the identification of the contractual terms to the tax consequences, in a readily accessible fashion.

I commend Julian on writing a book that covers so much in such a slim volume. It will be of considerable help to those who have to deal with employment law problems, be they lawyers, human resources personnel, trade union officials or the general public. There will be many in each of those categories who, for the first time, will appreciate the difference between unfair and wrongful dismissal and the interrelationship between the two.

Peter Kirby
Barrister
Hardwicke Building Employment Law Team, Lincoln's Inn

Preface

Employment law has developed and evolved in many respects in recent years. The proliferation of employment legislation, whether emanating from Westminster or from the European Parliament as a consequence of the United Kingdom's membership of the European Communities, presents a challenge to employment law advisors. Keeping abreast of regular changes to employment law is now the staple diet of employment lawyers in the current legal climate. The impact of these developments on businesses and employment rights in the workplace cannot be underestimated.

A recent survey revealed that, in 1990, there were 44,377 tribunal applications. This figure has risen to 118,400 in 2000, an increase of more than 100 per cent. Although the qualifying period for employees to bring an unfair dismissal claim was reduced in 1999 from two years to one year, employees without the requisite length of service may still be able to bring a claim for wrongful dismissal if the employer has committed a breach of contract. Wrongful dismissal claims may also be instituted where the aggrieved party is not an employee but renders services as a consultant or independent contractor, or where an employee falls within an excluded category to sue for unfair dismissal or where the damages sought by the employee are in excess of the current statutory maximum of £51,700 for unfair dismissal.

Employees are becoming more aware of their employment rights as a consequence of publicised cases and access to information on employment issues. The availability of 'No Win No Fee' arrangements is now widespread and increasingly used by employees as a means of funding litigation instituted against their former employer. Costs are rarely awarded against a losing party in tribunal proceedings so employees have nothing to lose in taking a gamble. New tribunal rules have been introduced by the government to curb unmeritorious claims by empowering tribunals to impose costs sanctions of up to £10,000 (previously £500) on employees who bring frivolous claims. These new tribunal rules are expected to be effective as of 16 July 2001. With effect from 21st February 2001, however, Tribunals may require employees to pay a deposit of £500 (previously £150) to the Tribunal as a condition for pursuing a weak case. Legal aid for employment tribunal proceedings has been introduced in Scotland as of 15 January 2001 and may become available in England and Wales in the future as a result of Article 6 of the European Convention of Human Rights now incorporated in the Human Rights Act 1998.

Against this litigious landscape and compensation culture, it is paramount that employers ensure that workplace practices are lawful. This will not only avoid unnecessary litigation, costs and time for the employer in the long term but reduce labour turnover and improve industrial relations.

The aim of this book is twofold: to ensure that employers' economic interests are adequately protected and that the rights of employees in the workplace are not infringed. Practical guidance for employers is highlighted with the △ symbol and tips for employees are emphasised with the ☞ symbol. I hope that this book and all the useful links contained herein will prove to be a valuable source of guidance for those advising employers and employees across a spectrum of industries.

I have endeavoured to state the law as it stands as at 1 June 2001. Any errors which remain in the book are my responsibility alone.

Julian Yew
Solicitor
Hextall Erskine

Acknowledgements

To my siblings Paul, Doris, Gordon and Laura for their encouragement and enduring support during my years in law school. To my partner, Rob, for putting up with my neglect as I worked ceaselessly through the evenings and weekends to see this publication to fruition. To Steve Reed and Janet Noble from the Law Society for their interest in this book. I am indebted to Chris Harrington for his technical contribution and for updating me on the proliferation of cases and legal developments emanating from the employment tribunals, courts, Parliament and the European Union and to Peter Kirby for his technical precision.

Table of cases

Table of statutes

Table of statutory instruments and European legislation

STATUTORY INSTRUMENTS

EUROPEAN LEGISLATION

CHAPTER 1

Unfair and wrongful dismissal

The legal concepts governing unfair dismissal and wrongful dismissal are not easily discernible to the layperson. The basis of each action and the remedies that are available in each case are separate and distinct but they are not mutually exclusive. Although the focus of this book is on wrongful dismissal, it is essential for every reader to appreciate the relationship between wrongful and unfair from the outset. In practice, it is common for both claims to be brought by an employee against the employer in one action.

1.1   UNFAIR DISMISSAL

Origins

This is a *statutory* claim pursuant to the Employment Rights Act 1996 (Part X s.94 ERA 1996 as amended). An employer may lawfully dismiss an employee if the reason for dismissal is one of the five substantive reasons permitted by law. These include misconduct, incapability, redundancy, illegality and 'some other substantial reason' (s.98 ERA 1996 as amended).

△   ILLEGALITY

> The Tribunal makes a distinction between a contract that is unlawful from the outset (e.g. to perform an illegal act or to carry out an immoral purpose) so that it is unenforceable by the parties and a contract that is tainted by illegality as a result of the employer's conduct but unknown to the employee (e.g. where the employer fails to deduct tax from the employee's remuneration). Thus, an employee who knowingly defrauds the Inland Revenue (*Napier* v. *National Business*

1

Agency [1951] 2 All ER 264) or works without a work permit (*Sharma v. Trustees and Executive Committee Members for the Time Being of the Hindu Cultural Society Slough* unreported, EAT 253/90) cannot enforce the contract for pursue his employment protection rights. Note however that an employee may still sue the employer for discrimination as such a claim is not dependent on the enforceability of the contract (*Leighton* v. *Michael; Leighton* v. *Charalambous* [1996] IRLR 67, *Hall* v. *Woolston Hall Leisure Ltd*, IDS Brief 664).

Even if an employer is able to establish a fair reason for dismissal, he is additionally required to act fairly in bringing about the dismissal (s.98(4) ERA 1996 as amended). Fairness depends on 'whether in the circumstances (including the size and administrative resources of the employer's undertaking) the employer acted reasonably or unreasonably in treating [the reason] as a sufficient reason for dismissing the employee and . . . [this] shall be determined in accordance with equity and the substantial merits of the case'.

Different considerations apply in respect of each of the five substantive reasons when deciding whether the employer has acted with procedural fairness.

Misconduct dismissals

Is the employee guilty of gross conduct justifying summary dismissal? Even so, summary dismissal is not synonymous to instant dismissal. The reasonableness of dismissal is two-fold.

Firstly, an employer is required to hold an honest belief that the employee is guilty of the misconduct, possess reasonable grounds for that belief and to have carried out reasonable investigations for that belief (*Midland Bank plc* v. *Madden* [2000] 2 All ER 741, CA). The employer is required to invoke its disciplinary and grievance procedure (Employment Code of Practice (Disciplinary and Grievance Procedures) Order 2000), ensuring that the employee is accompanied by a fellow colleague or union official, to investigate the matter (s.13 Employment Relations Act 1999). Even if the employee has admitted the misconduct, the employer is still under a duty to follow a fair procedure (*Whitbread plc (t/a Whitbread Medway Inns)* v. *Hall* [2001], EWCA Civ 268). Where the employer's disciplinary code allows the employer a discretion to dismiss, then other penalties apart from dismissal should be considered in the exercise of the discretion. Only in exceptional cases where, for example, the 'offence is so heinous and the facts so manifestly clear, that a reasonable employer could take the view that whatever the explanation the employee advanced it would make no difference' (*Polkey* v. *A.E. Dayton Services Ltd* [1987] AC 344, HL).

Secondly, the Employment Tribunal, whilst mindful that its role is not to substitute the view of the employer for its own view, will decide whether a reasonable employer would have done what the employer has done to the employee ('the band of reasonable responses') (*Iceland Frozen Foods Ltd* v. *Jones* [1982] IRLR 439, EAT, *Higgins* v. *C.R. Reynolds* ET 1801429/00). The band of reasonable responses for determining the fairness of a dismissal will apply to the sanction applied by the employer as well as the process by which the employer arrived at the decision to dismiss (*Whitbread plc (t/a Whitbread Medway Inns)* v. *Hall* [2001] EWCA Civ 268).

Where the misconduct is not gross, oral and written warnings may be necessary before dismissal. Employees should be told what standard of behaviour is expected of them (*John Lewis plc* v. *Coyne* [2001] IRLR 139). Previous warnings which have been excised from the employee's record should not be taken into account when a decision has to be taken on dismissal (*White* v. *Newsquest (Stourbridge) Ltd* unreported, 17 January 2001, EAT). The company's disciplinary code on conduct should set out what types of misconduct will lead to dismissal (e.g. misuse of the company's internet facilities, excessive use of the company's telephone for private calls, unauthorised absences). The employer should also ensure that there is uniformity of treatment in respect of unacceptable behaviour.

In respect of conduct outside the workplace (for example, drug taking, alcoholism, violent behaviour and criminal offences), they should only be taken into account if they bear some relation to the employee's position at work. If the employee is unable to fit in at work because of personality clashes with other workers, appropriate warnings should be dispensed to all parties concerned. Where, after reasonable investigation, the employer is still unable to pinpoint the culprit, it may be necessary to dismiss all parties who are involved in a serious misconduct rather than singling out one employee to be the scapegoat (*Monie* v. *Coral Racing Ltd* [1980] ICR 109, CA, *Parr* v. *Whitbread (t/a Thresher Wine Merchants)* [1990] ICR 427, EAT).

☞ Employees should note that the role of the Employment Tribunal is not to clear the name of the employee accused of the misconduct but to determine whether the employer had a fair reason for dismissal and had acted fairly in bringing about that dismissal

Incapability: illness and lack of skills

It is important to draw a distinction between incapability by reason of absence and lack of qualification or skill.

In respect of employee absenteeism, the employer should ascertain if the employee is malingering or genuinely ill. Malingerers should be dealt with using the misconduct guidelines, but those employees who are absent from work due to illness must be assessed separately.

In respect of absence due to illness, the employer should try to obtain a medical report from the employee's GP and then arrange for an examination by the company doctor. The employee must first consent to the release of their medical records but the employer should ensure that the employee is aware that withholding consent unreasonably may lead to the employer taking disciplinary action including dismissal. Employers should note that the employee has a legal right to examine the medical report before it is released to the employer (Access to Medical Reports Act 1988). The employer should then assess the severity of the employee's condition including the likelihood of recovery and, where possible, consider whether there is any suitable alternative employment within the company to accommodate the employee's health. Warnings are unsuitable in respect of such absences. The employer may be able to plead frustration (see 2.1) but the courts are reluctant to regard the contract as having come to an end this way as it would leave the employee with no protection. Where the employee's illness is a 'disability' within the Disability Discrimination Act 1995, the employer may be required to make necessary adjustments unless the failure can be justified.

⌂   In cases of chronic or long term sickness, employers should :

- consult with the employee;
- establish the true medical position including whether the employee is suffering from a disability;
- consider alternative employment.

Where the incapability arises from a lack of skill or qualification, the employer is required to consider offering training and supervision to the employee, setting reasonable targets and time for improvement, with a view to assisting the employee. The degree of such assistance depends on the size and administrative resources of the employer. A single act of incompetence may justify dismissal where the safety of the public or other workers is compromised (*Alidair* v. *Taylor* [1978] IRLR 82).

⚠ Note:

- Employers should draw a distinction between long term absences caused by an underlying medical condition and repeated or inter mittent absences caused by transient complaints;
- Employers who dismiss employees for 'misconduct' or 'incapability' should have regard to 'procedural fairness' as set out in the ACAS Code of Practice on Disciplinary and Grievance - Procedure 2000.

(www.acas.org.uk/12335_cofp.pdf)

Redundancy

The employer must ensure that it warns the employee of an imminent redundancy and consults with the employee prior to dismissal. If redundancy is unavoidable, the employer is required to consider whether there may be suitable alternative employment for the employee in the employer's parent and associated companies (*Williams* v. *Compair Maxim Limited* [1982] IRLR 83, EAT).

In respect of objective selection of candidates for redundancy, the employer should use a fair method of selection and factors to be taken into account include length of service, productivity, punctuality, disciplinary record, adaptability and the employer's future needs. Small employers are also required to adopt a fair process and this may include the application of the 'last-in first-out' rule. It is important to ensure that any criterion used is not indirectly discriminatory (for example, pregnancy or part-time working). The Court of Appeal recently held (*Whiffen* v. *Milham Ford Girls School* (2001) *The Times*, 3 April, CA) that a redundancy policy adopted by a school whereby a female employee working under a fixed term contract was deprived of an opportunity to be considered in the redundancy avoidance selection process, unlike male employees on permanent contracts, was indirectly discriminatory in the absence of justification.

The selection criteria adopted and consultation exercise should be documented. It is useful to note that a letter from an employer warning of impending redundancy will not constitute either consultation or an invitation to consult (*Rowell* v. *Hubbard Group Services Ltd* [1995] IRLR 195, EAT).

In respect of collective redundancies, there is a statutory duty to consult, failing which the employer may be liable to pay a protective award to the affected employees in accordance with the consultation periods listed below (s.190 Trade Union and Labour Relations (Consolidation) Act 1992). An employer who is proposing to make 20–99 employees redundant within 90 days must consult with the employees 30 days before the dismissal. In the case of 100 or more employees being made redundant within 90 days, there is a duty to consult 90 days in advance of the dismissal. The purpose of consultation is for the employer to disclose to the employee/employee's representative the reason for dismissal, the number of employees affected and the proposed method of selection for redundancy (s.188(4) Trade Union and Labour Relations (Consolidation) Act 1992). The employer and employee's representative will then try to agree on ways in which dismissals may be avoided (e.g. providing alternative employment, withdrawing contracted out work, introducing early retirement, relocating production, stopping recruitment and overtime), reducing the number of employees to be dismissed and mitigating the effects of dismissal. Failure to consult may render the employer liable to pay out a protective award based on a week's pay in respect of the consultation period. The 'protected period' is what is considered to be just and equitable having regard to the loss of days of consultation and the seriousness of the employer's default, up to a period of 90 days.

    ⌂   Whether a job is 'suitable' is a question of fact and an employee's unreasonable refusal of a job offer may result in a loss of the right to claim statutory redundancy payment.

'Some other substantial reason'

An employer may reorganise itself to improve business efficiency and this may lead to a change in employees' terms and conditions of employment. An employee who unreasonably refuses to co-operate with changes that are beneficial to the employer's interest may be dismissed. An employer must, however, ensure that proposed changes are not indirectly discriminatory (e.g. hiring only full time workers). In respect of employees who are unable to fit in or have personality clashes, the employer should consider transferring the employee as an option.

Who can claim unfair dismissal?

Only employees with one year of service with the employer and who are below the normal retirement age (statutory limit is 65 in the absence of a contractual retirement age) have a right to claim unfair dismissal. Certain categories of employees are excluded and these include constabulary members of the police service, offshore fishermen and employees of the Crown. As of 16 July 2001, Crown employees including the intelligence and security services (but not members of the police force) may be able to issue proceedings in Employment Tribunals, although such proceedings will be heard before a specially constituted tribunal (Employment Tribunals (Constitution and Rules of Procedure) Regulations 2001; Sched. 2, Employment Relations Act 1999 (Commencement No. 8) Order 2001). Where the interests of national security are at stake, the Advocate General may appoint a special advocate to act for the Applicant.

☞ Note however that employees who are 'ordinarily working outside Great Britain' may no longer be precluded from bringing a claim (s.196 of the ERA 1996 has been repealed by s.32 of the Employment Relations Act 1999 (ERA 1999)). The position of 'foreign workers' is now protected under the Contracts (Applicable Law) Act 1990 and the Directive on Posted Workers. For more information see *www.dti.gov.uk/er/section32.htm*

Where the dismissal is for an inadmissible reason (s.108 ERA 1996 as amended), i.e. where the employee has been dismissed for:

- a union related reason including trade union recognition or bargaining unit arrangements or taking part in a protected industrial action;
- the assertion of a statutory right under the Employment Rights Act 1996 including the right not to be unfairly dismissed and statutory minimum notice;
- a health and safety reason;
- a maternity reason;
- performing functions as a trustee of a pension scheme or an employee representative;
- a working time reason under the Working Time Regulations 1998;
- insisting on the right to a minimum wage under the National Minimum Wage Act 1998 (s. 104A ERA 1996);

7

- making a protected disclosure under the Public Interest Disclosure Act 1998 (s. 103A ERA 1996);
- exercising the right to accompany or be accompanied to a disci plinary or grievance hearing (s.10 Employment Relations Act 1999);
- time off for dependants;

no qualifying period is needed and the dismissal is *automatically unfair.*

Limitation period

Unfair dismissal claims must be instituted within three months from the effective date of termination (s.111(2)(a) ERA 1996). Applications out of time may be heard if it was not reasonably practicable for the complainant to bring a claim within the time limit (s.111(2)(b) ERA 1996). It has been held by the EAT that the onus is on the *employee* to show that it had not been reasonably practicable ('the feasibility test') to present the claim timeously and that this is a question of fact (*HFC Bank* v. *Hartley* unreported, 25 January 2001, EAT). A tribunal should not consider the length or reasonableness of the delay or whether it is 'just and equitable' to allow an out of time application in applying the feasibility test. Once it has been accepted that this is the case, the tribunal then has a discretion to accept an application out of time.

△ Where the employee has been dismissed with notice or has resigned with notice, the effective date of termination is when the notice expires (s.97 ERA 1996 as amended). Time starts to run against the employee from the effective date of termination.

Forum

Unfair dismissal claims are heard before a Tribunal chairperson and two lay members, one of whom has management experience and the other trade union experience. An employee has to institute proceedings in the 'home court' of the employer.

The employee (applicant) must lodge his complaint (application) using an ET1 Form. Upon receipt, the employer (Respondent) has 21 days to respond and then file his defence (Notice of Appearance) within 21 days using the ET3 Form.

📖 For free ET forms, see *www.emplaw.co.uk*. Note however that changes to the existing forms are anticipated so that in future, applicants would be required to 'particularise' the basis of their claim.

As of 16 July 2001, the Employment Tribunal has an 'overriding objective' to deal with cases justly. This requires Tribunals to ensure that parties are on an equal footing, parties are saving expense, cases are handled in a manner proportionate to the complexity of the issues and that cases are dealt with expeditiously and fairly (Sched. 1 r. 10 Employment Tribunals (Constitution and Rules of Procedure) Regulations 2001).

An Employment Tribunal may, as part of its case management powers, on its own motion or on application, issue directions as to the conduct of a case (Sched. 1 r. 4(1) Employment Tribunals (Constitution and Rules of Procedure) Regulations 2001). It also has miscellaneous powers to strike out an employee's claim or employer's notice of appearance if it is of the view that it is scandalous, misconceived or vexatious (Sched. 1 r. 15(2)(c) Employment Tribunals (Constitution and Rules of Procedure) Regulations 2001; *De Keyser Ltd* v. *Wilson* [2001] IRLR 324, EAT) or if the employee's claim is for want of prosecution (Sched. 1 r. 15(2)(e) Employment Tribunals (Constitution and Rules of Procedure) Regulations 2001). The chairman of the Employment Tribunal may require a party to provide further information, give disclosure of documents, require a witness to attend a hearing by way of a Witness Order (even on the Tribunal's own motion (*Clapson* v. *British Airways plc* [2001] IRLR 184)) or require one party to answer questions in writing (Sched. 1 r. 4(3) and (5) Employment Tribunals (Constitution and Rules of Procedure) Regulations 2001). If directions are not complied with, the Tribunal has powers to strike out an application or notice of appearance if the party in default fails to show cause for the non-compliance or make an order for costs (Sched. 1 r. 4(8) Employment Tribunals (Constitution and Rules of Procedure) Regulations 2001).

Either party may make an application to the Employment Tribunal for a Pre-hearing Review (PHR) where an application or any issue contended has no reasonable prospect of success (Sched. 1 r. 7(1) Employment Tribunals (Constitution and Rules of Procedure) Regulations 2001). A PHR is usually heard by a Chairman alone. Although the PHR is designed to weed out weak claims and defences, evidence is not adduced in such a hearing which renders the procedure of limited use in practice. A party who is insistent on carrying on with the case may be required to pay a deposit within 21 days as a condition for pursuing the case (Sched. 1 r. 7(7) Employment Tribunals (Constitution and Rules of Procedure) Regulations 2001). Further, the party bears the risk of a costs order awarded against him/her in the event of defeat at the hearing. As of 21 February 2001, Tribunals are empowered to require employees to pay a deposit of up to £500 (previously £150) as a condition of pursuing a claim in weak cases (The Employment Tribunals (Increase of Maximum Deposit) Order 2001).

Costs are rarely awarded in tribunal proceedings unless one party (applicant or respondent) has acted vexatiously, abusively, disruptively or unreasonably. It is envisaged that as of 16 July 2001, an Employment Tribunal may impose a costs order of up to £10,000 (Sched. 1 r. 14(3) Employment Tribunals (Constitution and Rules of Procedure) Regulations 2001).

Proceedings may be stayed by the Employment Tribunal if there are concurrent proceedings issued in the High Court arising from the same employment.

An Employment Tribunal may review, vary or revoke its own decision where an error has been made, where the decision has been made in the absence of a party, where new evidence becomes available after the decision or the interest of justice requires a review (Sched. 1 r. 13(1) Employment Tribunals (Constitution and Rules of Procedure) Regulations 2001). An application must be made within 14 days from the date of the decision.

Appeals from the decision of an Employment Tribunal lie to the Employment Appeals Tribunal (EAT). A Notice of Appeal in Form 1 must be made within 42 days from the date the tribunal's decision was sent to the appellant (r. 3 Employment Appeal Tribunal Rules 1993). Legal funding is available for appeals to the EAT subject to means. Appeals from the EAT lie to the Court of Appeal and must be made within 4 weeks from the written decision of the EAT.

Remedies

An employee who has been unfairly dismissed may ask the Tribunal for an Order requiring the employer to:

- reinstate them (give them back their old job);

- re-engage them (give them another job within the company);
- award them damages.

Orders for reinstatement and re-engagement are subject to whether it is practical for the employer to do so and whether the employee has contributed to the dismissal. Where the relationship of trust and confidence has broken down, these remedies may not be possible.

The award of damages for unfair dismissal is based on *'such amount as the tribunal considers just and equitable in all the circumstances, having regard to the loss sustained by the complainant as a result of the dismissal'* (s.123(1) ERA 1996).

☞ In respect of monetary compensation, the employee will be entitled to a:

- *basic award* calculated by reference to a week's pay, the age of the employee and the number of years the employee has worked. The current maximum for a week's pay is £240. The current maximum for a basic award is £7,200 (Employment Rights (Increase of Limits) Order 2001), (20 years × 240 per week × 1.5 multiplier). See the 'ready reckoner' found at the Appendix 1.

- *compensatory award* which comprises immediate and future loss of earnings, loss of use of company car/mobile phone, loss of benefits in kind and loss of statutory rights. The current maximum is £51,700 where the effective date of termination is on/after 1 February 2001 (the maximum is £50,000 for employees whose effective date of termination is on/after 25 October 1999 and up to 31 January 2001). This financial ceiling is likely to be of significance to higher income employees earning between £50,000 to £100,000 p.a.

⚠ The Basic Award may be reduced if the employee has unreasonably refused reinstatement, been guilty of a misconduct prior to dismissal or has received a redundancy payment. For employees aged between 64 and 65, it also reduces by 1/12th for every completed month by which the age exceeds 64.

⚠ The Compensatory Award may be reduced if the employee has received monies in lieu of notice, found alternative employment or contributed to their own dismissal.

Interest at 15 per cent is payable on any award by an Employment Tribunal which remains unpaid 42 days after the Tribunal's decision has been sent to the parties (Industrial Tribunal (Interest) Order 1990). Note that interest continues to run even when one party has lodged an appeal. If the employee has been successful in an appeal, interest only commences when the Employment Appeals Tribunal has made the Order.

1.2   WRONGFUL DISMISSAL

This is a common law claim for breach of contract.

Who can claim for wrongful dismissal?

Any employee may sue for wrongful dismissal if any term in the contract, whether expressly agreed between the parties or implied by custom, statute or collective agreement, has been breached. Independent contractors and consultants may sue for wrongful termination of the contract. There is no qualifying period or age limit in such a claim.

Limitation period

Employees have three months from the effective date of termination to bring a claim for wrongful dismissal in the Employment Tribunal (art. 7 Employment Tribunals Extension of Jurisdiction (England and Wales) Order 1994) provided a claim exists or is outstanding on the termination of employment (art. 3(c) Employment Tribunals Extension of Jurisdiction (England and Wales) Order 1994). Unlike unfair dismissal, the employer may counterclaim but has to do so within six weeks from the date of receipt of the employee's application (art. 8 Employment Tribunals Extension of Jurisdiction (England and Wales) Order 1994).

The time limit for bringing wrongful dismissal/termination claims in the county court or High Court is six years from the date of the breach of contract.

Forum

Claims of up to £25,000 may be brought in the Employment Tribunal. The Employment Tribunal has no power to award damages in excess of £25,000. Any attempts by an employee to recover the excess in the civil courts may be defended on the grounds of estoppel or an abuse of process. The Employment Tribunal does not have jurisdiction to hear complaints in respect of terms relating to restrictive covenants, intellectual property, confidence, service accommodation and damages for personal injuries. Such complaints would have to be issued in the county court or High Court (art. 5 Employment Tribunals Extension of Jurisdiction (England and Wales) Order 1994).

△ Apart from the above limitations, an employee may sue the employer for wrongful dismissal in either the civil courts or the Employment Tribunal. The six year limitation period in respect of breach of contract claims in the civil courts may prove useful to an employee who is time barred from Employment Tribunal proceedings.

Claims of £25,000 or more may be instituted in the county court or High Court. There is a criteria for the transfer of cases between the county court and the High Court. This will depend on the financial value of the claim and the complexity of the issues among other things (Rule 30.3(2) CPR 1998). Procedures in the civil courts are more formal than those in the Employment Tribunal and are governed by the Civil Procedural Rules.

The Civil Procedural Rules 1998 (CPR) came into force on 1 April 1999. These rules apply to proceedings in both the county court and High Court. The aim of the CPR is to enable the courts to deal with cases justly and this means involving the courts in actively managing cases (Part 1 CPR 1998). Claims of less than £5,000 are dealt with in the Small Claims track (Part 27 CPR 1998), claims up to £15,000 in the Fast track (Part 28 CPR 1998) and claims in excess of £15,000 in the Multi track (Part 29 CPR 1998). Proceedings in the civil courts may be commenced by way of a Part 7 Claim. Claimants should use Form N1. The court issue fees are as shown in Tables 1–3.

Table 1 Commencement of proceedings

To recover a sum of money in the County Court:

Less than £500	£60
Less than £1,000	£80
Less than £5,000	£115
Less than £15,000	£230
Less than £50,000	£350
More than £50,000	£500
For any other remedy	£120
Filing a Listing Questionnaire:	
multi track	£300
other tracks	£200

To recover a sum of money in the High Court:

Less than £50,000	£350
More than £50,000	£500
For any other remedy	£120
Filing a Listing Questionnaire	£400

County Court and High Court fees:

Claimant filing	
Allocation Questionnaire	£80
Application for Consent Order	£25
Application notices	£50

Table 2 Fixed costs on commencement of a claim (Rule 45.2(2) Civil Procedural Rules 1998

Value	Claim form served by court	Claim form served by claimant	Claim form served by claimant where there is more than one defendant
£25.01–£500	£50	£60	Add £15
£500.01–£1,000	£70	£80	Add £15
£100.01–£5,000	£80	£90	Add £15
Over £5,000	£100	£110	Add £15

Table 3 Fixed costs on entry of judgment (Rule 45.4 CPR)

	Where judgment exceeds £25 but less than £5,000	Where judgment exceeds £5,000
Default judgement—Failure to file AOS	£22	£30
Default judgement—Failure to file defence	£25	£35
Judgment entered on admission of part or entire claim and claimant accepts defendant's proposal for payment	£40	£55
Judgment entered on admission of part/entire claim and court decides on mode of payment	£55	£70
Summary judgment	£175	£210

Particulars of claim may be attached to the claim form or served separately within 14 days from the date of the claim form.

Once the defendant has received the Claimant's Statement of Case, they have 14 days to file an Acknowledgment of Service (AOS) in Form N9 (Part 7 claim). If an AOS has been filed at court, the defendant has 28 days from the date of receipt of the claimant's claim to file a defence. The defendant may either admit the whole of the claimant's claim, admit part of the claim or dispute the entire claim using Form N9A or file a defence and counterclaim using Form N9B. If the defendant has a counterclaim (Part 20 CPR), Form N9B should be used. The claimant should file an AOS in respect of the defendant's counterclaim using Form N213.

When a defence has been filed, the court will send out an Allocation Questionnaire in Form N150 requesting information on whether experts are needed, the number of witnesses, proposed directions, attempts to settle and likely costs incurred and allocate the case to the relevant track. A claimant who files an Allocation Questionnaire is required to pay a court fee.

If the defendant does not file an AOS or a defence, the claimant may ask the court for default judgment (Part 12 CPR). Where a defence has been filed but is unmeritorious, the claimant may ask the court for summary judgment (Part 24 CPR). Where the claimant's claim is frivolous, the defendant may ask the court to strike out the claimant's action (Rule 3.4 CPR)

Interim applications may be commenced by using Form N244 (Application Notice) if either party needs an Order from the court in respect of specific disclosure and any other directions as the case may be.

Before a case is set down for trial, the court may require the parties to file a Listing Questionnaire. This is to enable the court to establish if directions have been complied with, if experts will be testifying, the number of witnesses to be called, if the parties are legally represented and an estimate of how long the trial will take. A claimant who files a Listing Questionnaire is required to pay a court fee.

Costs are awarded in the civil courts. There are fixed costs allowed on the issue of a claim and on entry of judgment where a party is represented by a solicitor (Part 45 CPR). There are also costs in respect of the outcome of an interlocutory application or the case itself (Part 47 CPR). These are either summarily assessed at the end of hearings (parties are expected to provide a breakdown to the judge) or subject to detailed assessment at a later stage by a costs judge. In respect of the latter, the person entitled to costs serves a notice of commencement of assessment in Form N252 and the paying party has 21 days to file any point of dispute. If no dispute is raised, the court may issue a default costs certificate in Form N255. If points of dispute are served, then the costs judge will convene a detailed assessment hearing and deal with those issues in dispute and award a final costs certificate in Form N256. Assessed costs are rarely awarded in the Small Claims track.

A significant development of the CPR is the introduction of offers to settle and payments into court (Part 36 CPR). Either the claimant or the defendant may make use of the Part 36 procedure to attempt to reach a settlement without recourse to full trial. The costs implications of failing to beat a payment into court act as an impetus for the parties to abort the need for the dispute to proceed to a full blown trial (see 7.4)

Pre-action protocols were introduced under the CPR to promote early exchange of information between the parties including the issues in dispute and evidence without the need to commence proceedings. There are currently Protocols in respect of personal injury, construction, defamation and clinical negligence. A draft Pre-action protocol in respect of employment disputes has been submitted to the Lord

Chancellor's Department for consideration by the Employment Lawyers' Association working party. It is envisaged that this will apply to wrongful termination claims by both employees and workers.

Appeals from the county court lie to the High Court. Appeals from the High Court lie to the Court of Appeal.

For further information on court forms, rules and practice directions, go to *www.courtservice.gov.uk*.

Remedies

Damages for wrongful dismissal are limited to what the aggrieved party would have got had the contract been performed. Only damages within the reasonable contemplation of the parties at the time of contract are recoverable and the injured party is required to mitigate their losses. However, damages for wrongful dismissal are normally confined to the notice period which would be the time when an employer may lawfully terminate a contract or, as the case may be, the balance of a fixed term contract if there is no break clause. Unlike unfair dismissal, there is no financial limit on the level of damages. Although contributory conduct is irrelevant in the assessment of damages for wrongful dismissal, the employee is expected to mitigate their losses so that any earnings from the employee's new employment must be accounted for.

Where judgment has been obtained, interest at 8 per cent starts to run against the losing party from the date of judgment (s.69 County Courts Act 1984 and s.35A Supreme Court Act 1981) until the judgment is satisfied.

CHAPTER 2

Terminations and dismissals

A dismissal may stem from a termination of contract but not all terminations amount to a dismissal. A contract may be terminated in various ways as set out below but an employee is only regarded as being dismissed at law within certain prescribed circumstances.

For the avoidance of doubt, only employees under a contract of service may be dismissed under the Employment Rights Act 1996. Non-employees such as independent contractors and consultants, who work pursuant to a contract for service may, following a breach of contract, sue for wrongful termination.

2.1   TERMINATIONS

A contract of employment may be terminated in the ways outlined below.

Mutual consent of the parties

Either party may agree to terminate and release the other from continuing obligations under the contract of employment. For example, some employees may be willing to accept early retirement (*University of Liverpool* v. *Humber and Birch* [1985] ICR 470) or a voluntary redundancy package in excess of what is ordinarily payable. A resignation is not a dismissal but see 2.2 on constructive dismissal. Where a contract provides that if an employee does not return to work upon the expiry of their leave, and that such absence would automatically terminate the contract, the courts have refused to recognise the event as termination by mutual consent but a dismissal (*Igbo* v. *Johnson Matthey Chemicals* [1986] IRLR 215). An employee may resign but cannot be deemed to have dismissed himself. The law no longer recognises the concept of 'constructive resignation' (*London Transport Executive v. Clarke* [1981] IRLR 166).

Completion of specific task

If a contract has been entered into for the performance of a specific task and the task is duly completed, the contract will be terminated accordingly. An employer may also stipulate that a contract will come to an end on the occurrence of a specified event, otherwise known as a 'condition subsequent'. For example, a contract may be terminated when funding for a position ceases (*Brown v. Knowsley Borough Council* [1986] IRLR 102) or when an employee who has been absent from work returns after maternity leave.

Death of employer or employee

If either party to the contract dies before or during the currency of the contract, the contract is deemed to be terminated (s.133(1) ERA 1996).

Insolvency of the employer

Where an employer becomes insolvent, the contract of employment is deemed to have been terminated (s.182(1) ERA 1996). If an employee is being owed any arrears of pay of less than eight weeks, statutory notice pay, holiday pay of less than six weeks or any basic award for compensation for unfair dismissal, he/she may make a claim against the Secretary of State out of the National Insurance Fund (s.182 Employment Rights Act 1996).

Frustration

A contract may be terminated by way of frustration at common law. This occurs when an unforeseen event, through no fault of the parties, makes future performance of the contract illegal, impossible or radically different from what was contemplated by the parties. A contract may be frustrated when an employee has been imprisoned for a criminal offence for a considerable period of time and is therefore unable to work (*Harrington v. Kent County Council* [1980] IRLR 353) and that it is not commercially practical for the employer to hire a temporary worker (*Chakki* v. *United Yeast Co Ltd* [1982] ICR 140). A contract may also be frustrated where an employee is absent for long periods due to sickness (*Williams v Watsons Luxury Coaches* [1990] IRLR 164) although the courts are reluctant to apply the doctrine of frustration too easily in view of the Disability Discrimination Act 1995 and its potential abuse by employers to wriggle out of contractual obligations. It is not possible for employers to rely on a redundancy situation as a frustrating event as redundancy amounts to a dismissal at law in any event (see 2.2 'Redundancy').

At common law, where there is a frustrating event, the employer or employee has no right to claim anything unless there has been a total failure of consideration from either party (*Fibrosa Spolka Akcyjna* v. *Fairbairn Lawson Combe Barbour* [1943] AC 32). However, the Law Reform (Frustrated Contracts) Act 1943 (s.1(2) and 1(3) Law Reform (Frustrated Contracts) Act 1943) changed that position. It provides that any sum paid prior to a frustrating event is recoverable and any sum payable prior to a frustrating event ceased to be payable. The payee may be entitled to set off his expenses against the sums so paid. Where one party has conferred a 'valuable benefit' to the other party (other than a payment of money), he may claim a just sum not exceeding the value of that benefit.

If an employer has sponsored an employee to attend a full time course and the employee is paid while on the course but then is unable to continue with the course as a result of imprisonment or long term illness, the employer would arguably be able to claw back any payments made to the employee, stop any future payments and also deduct any expenses incurred in sponsoring the employee. Conversely, where the contract is frustrated by illegality, the employee may be able to claim a just sum if they have conferred a 'valuable benefit' to the employer. The employee's claim is not an enforcement of an illegal contract at common law but arguably the exercise of the employee's statutory rights pursuant to the 1943 Act.

2.2 DISMISSALS

At common law, a dismissal occurs when a contract is terminated by notice, without notice or where one party commits a fundamental breach of contract.

There are four types of situation giving rise to a dismissal at law for the purposes of unfair dismissal and redundancy (ss.95 and 136 ERA 1996).

Termination by the employer

Where the employer gives the employee notice of termination, the employee is deemed dismissed by the employer. The effective date of termination, for the purposes of calculating when the limitation period starts to run against the employee if they wish to institute legal proceedings, is when the notice period expires. Employees who are summarily dismissed for gross misconduct are not entitled to any notice period. A resignation under threat of dismissal may constitute dismissal provided that the threat is immediate and unambiguous (*Martin* v. *Glynwed Distribution* [1983] IRLR 198). Whether words said amount to a dismissal is subject to an objective test; would a reasonable person have understood the words to be tantamount to a dismissal? A dismissal once effected cannot generally be withdrawn. However, words said in the heat of the moment by the employer and retracted shortly afterwards may not give rise to a dismissal (*Martin* v. *Yeoman Aggregates* [1983] IRLR 49). The same principles should apply to a resignation.

△ Where the employer has given the employee notice of termination and the employee later gives their counter notice of termination to expire earlier than the employer's notice, there is still a dismissal at law (s.95(2)(b) ERA 1996). The effective date of termination is when the employee's counter notice expires. The concept of 'early notice' was introduced so that employees who have been made redundant and who have found new jobs to start before the expiry of the employer's notice, may leave early without being deemed to have resigned or mutually terminated the contract thereby losing the right to claim redundancy or unfair dismissal.

The effective date of termination (EDT) is dependent on the following:

- when an employee is summarily dismissed, the EDT is the day of dismissal;
- when notice of termination is given, the EDT is when the notice period expires;
- when notice of termination is given and the contract allows for payment in lieu of notice (PILON), the EDT is when the PILON

is made (*Rex Stewart Jefferies Parker Ginsberg Ltd* v. *Parker* [1988] IRLR 483, CA)

- when both the employer and employee agree that the contract will end forthwith on the payment of a PILON, the EDT is when the PILON is made.

Expiry of a fixed term contract

A fixed term contract must have a clear start and finish date although the presence of a break clause allowing either party to terminate the contract before the expiry of the fixed term does not preclude it from being a fixed term contract (*Dixon* v. *British Broadcasting Corporation* [1979] ICR 281). Non-renewal of a fixed term contract amounts to a dismissal (s.95(1)(b) ERA 1996). However, the issue is whether the dismissal is wrongful or unfair, without which the employee has no cause of action. The effective date of termination is when the fixed term contract expires.

Constructive dismissal and resignation

An employee is also deemed to be dismissed when 'the employee terminates the contract under which he is employed (with or without notice) in circumstances in which he is entitled to terminate it *without notice* by reason of the employer's conduct' (s.95(1)(c) ERA 1996).

Where the employer has committed a fundamental or repudiatory breach of contract, the employee may resign, with or without notice, and claim that he has been constructively dismissed. It has been held by the Court of Appeal that:

> If the employer is guilty of misconduct which is a significant breach going to the root of the contract of employment, or which shows that the employer no longer intends to be bound by one or more of the essential terms of the contract, then the employee is entitled to treat himself as discharged from any further performance. If he does so, then he terminates the contract by reason of the employer's conduct. He is constructively dismissed. The employee is entitled in those circumstances to leave at the instant without giving notice at all or, alternatively, he may give notice and say that he is leaving at the end of the notice. But the conduct must in either case be sufficiently serious to entitle him to leave at once (Western Excavating (ECC) Ltd v. Sharp [1978] ICR 221, CA, per Lord Denning MR) (the contractual test).

To claim constructive dismissal, the employee thus has to show that one of the express terms of the contract has been breached sufficiently to constitute repudiation, for example, unlawful reduction in pay, unlawful variation of job description and change of hours not permitted by the contract. However, the 'contractual test' has been developed over the years to include a breach of the implied term of mutual respect. Serious unreasonable conduct on the part of the employer may evidence a breach of trust and confidence (see 4.20 for examples).

An employee may rely on a single incident if it is sufficiently grave or a series of minor events which when taken together may constitute a fundamental breach. An employee should make it clear that the employer's conduct is not acceptable and that they are resigning in response to it. If the employee is resigning with notice, then they have to ensure that it is known to the employer that they are working under protest. So long as a causal link is established, a constructive dismissal can still be maintained even though the employee remains in the employ of the employer while waiting to secure another job (*Waltons and Morse* v. *Dorrington* [1997] IRLR 488).

⚖ Has the employer done anything which could be said to have destroyed the relationship of trust and confidence between the employer and the employee?

☞ It is important for employees to bear in mind that they have to show that the employer's conduct is unacceptable and that it amounts to a fundamental breach of contract entitling the employee to resign. For this reason, the employee has to make it clear to the employer why they are resigning, i.e. that the resignation is in response to the employer's repudiatory breach. Otherwise, the employer may turn around and say that the employee has resigned for some other reason unconnected with the employer's conduct (e.g. because the employee has found alternative employment). Thus, an employee is advised not simply to 'walk out' from the employer except in severe cases as this may prove to be premature and may give rise to causation problems in a constructive dismissal claim (*Norwest Holst Group Administration Ltd* v. *Harrison* [1985] ICR 668).

Where the employee is constructively dismissed with notice, the effective date of termination is when the notice period expires.

⚖☞ The concept of constructive dismissal applies to rights under the Employment Rights Act 1996, Sex Discrimination Act 1975 and

Race Relations Act 1976 but not the Disability Discrimination Act 1995 (*Commissioner of Police of the Metropolis* v. *Harley* [2001] IRLR 263, EAT).

Where the employee resigns for a reason unconnected with the employer's conduct, there is no deemed dismissal and therefore no right to claim unfair or wrongful dismissal. An employee who has resigned with notice remains an employee until the notice period expires (i.e. the effective date of termination). Arguably, such an employee may nonetheless be subject to summary dismissal during the notice period. If the employer does not accept the employee's resignation and there are no grounds for summary dismissal, the employer can only dismiss with notice otherwise the dismissal would be wrongful and potentially unfair. There is no statutory provision governing the service of a counter notice by an employer when an employee has resigned (compare with 2.2 'Termination by the employer').

Redundancy

Where a redundancy situation arises and the employee's employment is terminated, the employee is deemed to be dismissed by reason of redundancy (s.139(1) ERA 1996). For those who have continuity of service of two years prior to notice of redundancy, they will qualify for statutory redundancy payments in the absence of a contractual redundancy scheme. Whereas redundancy is a fair reason for dismissal (s. 98(2)(c) ERA 1996), the employer is still required to act fairly in bringing about the dismissal. This will entail warning affected employees in advance, applying an objective selection of candidates and consultation with the employees (see. 1.1 on redundancy).

CHAPTER 3

Terms of employment contracts

A contract of employment may be oral or in writing (s.230(2) ERA 1996). An oral contract is more difficult to prove in the event of a dispute.

3.1 EXPRESS TERMS

The express terms of a contract are those agreed between the parties. These terms often relate to the employee's job description, duration, salary, place of work, hours of work, holiday entitlement, bonuses, notice periods and disciplinary and grievance procedures. Parties may agree to any terms provided that the terms:

- are not discriminatory under the Equal Pay Act 1970, Sex Discrimination Act 1975, Race Relations Act 1976 and Disability Discrimination Act 1995;

- do not fall foul of the law (Reg. 12 Transfer of Undertakings (Protection of Employment) Regulations 1981 'TUPE') but note that it is possible to contract out of the right to claim unfair dismissal under Part X ERA 1996 which arguably includes dismissal for a TUPE reason under reg. 8(1) TUPE.

- do not exclude liability for death or personal injury caused by the employer's negligence (s.2(1) Unfair Contract Terms Act 1977 'UCTA');

- do not exclude an employee's right to claim unfair dismissal upon the expiry of a fixed term contract although it is possible to exclude the employee's right to a redundancy payment where the employee works under a fixed term contract of two years or more (s.18 Employment Relations Act 1999, s.203 ERA 1996).

⌂ S.3 UCTA 1997 provides that an express term which seeks to exclude or limit the liability of the employer in the performance of the contract, or to perform substantially differently from that reasonably expected of him, or to render no performance is only enforceable if it satisfies a reasonableness test. It was once accepted that this does not apply to contracts of employment but a recent High Court decision has held otherwise (*Brigden* v. *American Express Bank Ltd* [2000] IRLR 94). Any onerous terms may be deemed unenforceable under the Act. Employees should be asked to take independent legal advice as the courts will look at the bargaining positions when considering whether a term was reasonable at the time of contract.

Many employers have work rules, policies and company handbooks in the workplace. These may relate to equal opportunities, a 'no smoking' office environment, disciplinary and grievance procedures and retirement ages. If these rules and policies are for guidance only, then they do not form part of the contract. Thus, there is no breach of contract in the event of the employer departing from them (*Grant* v. *South West Trains Ltd* [1998] IRLR 206, ECJ) although a tribunal may take into account the employer's behaviour if it is called to decide if a dismissal is unfair.

⌂ An employer is required to provide an employee with a statutory statement of particulars of employment within two months of employment (s.1 ERA 1996) (see Appendix 3). While this is not necessarily a contract of employment, it may evidence the terms of agreement between the parties. Employers will need to include additional terms such as garden leave, confidentiality, inventions and other relevant benefits in the contract of employment.

3.2   IMPLIED TERMS

The law recognises that in employment relationships, there will always be an inequality of bargaining positions. Parliament and the courts therefore mitigate this imbalance by implying certain terms into a contract of employment to protect both the employer and employee.

Terms may be implied in the employment relationship to give the contract business efficacy or where a term is so obvious to the officious bystander it is deemed to be part of the agreement of the parties.

Terms may be implied by reason of the employer's custom, rules or conduct of the parties. Examples of such terms include whether holidays may be carried from one leave year to another, festive closures and overtime when the contract is silent on these matters.

Terms are also implied at common law. An employer is required to pay wages, to behave in a manner that does not destroy the relationship of trust and confidence and to ensure the health and safety of its employees. In some cases, an employer may be required to provide employees with work (*William Hill Organisation Ltd v. Tucker* [1998] IRLR 313, CA). An employee is required to act in to act in good faith towards the employer, to work diligently and with care and not to disclose trade secrets and confidential information. Both an employer and employee are required to provide reasonable notice for termination in the absence of express provision.

More importantly but often overlooked are terms which are implied by statute by way of Acts of Parliament and Statutory Instruments in the employment contract. These statutory implied terms include the Sex Discrimination Act 1975, Race Relations Act 1976 and Disability Discrimination Act 1995, Health and Safety at Work etc Act 1974, Working Time Regulations 1998, Public Interest Disclosure Act 1998, Employment Rights Act 1996, Part-time Workers (Prevention of Less Favourable Treatment) Regulations 2000, Human Rights Act 1998 and Telecommunication (Lawful Business Practice) (Interception of Communications) Regulations 2000. These implied terms are dealt with in more detail at 4.23.

3.3 COLLECTIVE AGREEMENTS

A collective agreement is a contract made between an employee's union and the employer or employer's association. Such an agreement does not have the force of law (s.179(1) Trade Union and Labour Relations (Consolidation) Act 1992) and is no more than a 'gentleman's agreement' to promote good industrial relations. An employee may have difficulty enforcing the terms agreed in the collective agreement as the employee is not privy to the collective agreement. However, this position has to some degree been mitigated by the Contracts (Rights of Third Parties) Act 1999 where a third party may now benefit from a contract even though they are not privy to the contract and have not provided consideration to the parties. However, this presupposes that the contract is valid at law to begin with.

27

Therefore, an employee who wishes to enforce any terms negotiated in a collective agreement would have to show that the terms were expressly or impliedly incorporated into the contract of employment. To avoid an innocent party being automatically bound to terms which have been negotiated by their trade union but unknown to the employee, the courts are only prepared to accept that such terms are incorporated if the employee is aware of them and has accepted the terms as part of the employment contract (*Sagar* v. *H Ridehalgh & Son Ltd* [1931] 1 Ch 310, CA). Collective terms may be impliedly incorporated by way of custom and practice applicable to the employee's employment (*London General Transport Services Ltd* v. *Henry* [2001] IRLR 132).

☞   Employees should check if terms negotiated in a collective agreement are part of the contract by requesting a s.1 written statement of particulars of employment (see Appendix 3).

CHAPTER 4

Breach of contract

A breach of contract occurs when a term of the contract is broken. The burden of proof rests on the party alleging that a breach has occurred. A breach may take the following forms.

4.1 FUNDAMENTAL BREACH

A fundamental breach occurs when one party shows by their conduct that they no longer wish to be bound by the terms of a contract, e.g. an employee who refuses to obey the employer's lawful and legitimate instruction commits a material breach of contract; this principle applies even if the employer has issued the instructions in bad faith (*Macari* v. *Celtic Football and Athletic Co Ltd* [1999] **IRLR** 787).

4.2 ANTICIPATORY/REPUDIATORY BREACH

An anticipatory breach occurs when one party indicates an intention not to be bound by the contract before performance has begun or in respect of future obligations (for example,the withdrawal of a job offer (*Hochster* v. *De La Tour* (1853) 2 **E&B** 678)).

A breach of contract does not automatically terminate a contract. A breach entitles the innocent party to various options. It:

• entitles the innocent party to recover damages in respect of the loss suffered from the breach;

• may prevent the guilty party from enforcing the obligations owed by the innocent party under the contract (see 6.6 on restrictive covenants);

- entitles the innocent party to accept the breach and terminate the contract (*Howard* v. *Pickford Tool Co Ltd* [1951] 1 KB 417) (for example, where the employee is guilty of gross misconduct, severe incompetence or failure to carry out his duties);

- entitles the innocent party to affirm the contract by insisting on performance of the contract.

If the innocent party elects to affirm the contract, he may still sue for damages in respect of the breach that has occurred. Once the innocent party has elected to affirm the contract, both parties remain bound to continue with the obligations under the contract.

In employment contracts, however, the right of an employee to insist on affirming the contract is not an absolute one. In the case of summary dismissal, the employee does not have a right of election and the termination is 'carved in stone' (*Sanders* v. *Neale Ernest A.*) [1974] ICR 565). There have been numerous cases where employees have been granted declarations or injunctions to prevent an employer acting in breach of its disciplinary procedure which supports the elective theory (*Dietmann* v. *Brent London Borough Council* [1987] ICR 737, *Gunton* v. *Richmond-upon-Thames London Borough Council* (No. 2) [1980] ICR 755). More recently, the Court of Appeal has cast doubt on the elective theory and criticised the application of the elective theory in employment contracts (*Boyo* v. *Lambeth London Borough Council* [1995] IRLR 50). The current view is that an employee does not have a right to insist on performance of the contract in the event of a breach (see 5.1 on the 'Lavarack principle').

To determine whether a breach of contract has occurred, you need to look at the terms of the contract and the circumstances giving rise to the termination.

4.3   WITHDRAWAL OF JOB OFFER BY EMPLOYER

Once a person has accepted an offer of employment, there is a binding contract and withdrawal of the job offer will constitute a breach of contract. An employer may withdraw an offer for various reasons e.g. due to receipt of an unsuitable reference from the employee's previous employer, re-organisation or discovering that the prospective employee may be suffering from poor health.

Technically, the employee will be entitled to notice pay (the period the employer would have had to give to the employee to terminate the contract). Where there is a fixed term contract with no break clause, the employer may be liable to compensate the employee for losses in respect of the unexpired term.

⚠ Make all effort to avoid the situation where a job offer must be withdrawn:

- plan ahead: what are the company's long term and short term needs? Can the vacancy be filled internally? There is no obligation on employers to advertise for jobs but selective informal consultation ('secret soundings') with a view to recruiting internally may give rise to a claim for sex discrimination (*Lord Chancellor v. Coker; Osamore v. Lord Chancellor* [2001] IRLR 116, EAT (on appeal to CA)). If you need to recruit externally, ensure that you get the right person for the job;

- ensure that it is clear that any job offer is conditional upon receipt of satisfactory references from the employee's former employer (*Wishart v. National Association of Citizens Advice Bureaux* [1990] IRLR 393). In the case of unsatisfactory references, reserve the right to terminate the contract (see Appendix 2 Offer Letter);

- chase up references promptly;

- if the job offer is withdrawn because of the job applicant's poor health, ensure that this does not constitute disability discrimination (s.5 Disability Discrimination Act 1995);

- where the employee is also offered a directorship, any appointment for a term exceeding five years must be approved by shareholders (s.319 Companies Act 1985). In the case of listed companies, the Combined Code of the London Stock Exchange recommends that approval is sought from shareholders for appointments in excess of one year.

☞ If a job offer is withdrawn:

- establish the reason for the withdrawal of the job offer;

- was anything asked or said during the interview which may have given cause for the employer's withdrawal? For example, was the employee asked about their marital status or if they were planning to start a family soon? This may constitute sex discrimination;

- did the employee declare that they had a disability in the application form or at the interview? Refusal to take someone on

31

because of the person's disability may be a breach of s.5 Disability Discrimination Act 1995.

4.4   WITHDRAWAL OF ACCEPTANCE BY EMPLOYEE

If the employee has accepted the job but decides subsequently not to accept the position, this amounts to a breach of contract by the employee. Employers who intend to sue such employees must show that they have suffered a loss, e.g. the costs of advertising again and recruiting someone else. Often, employers can simply select the next best candidate who had been shortlisted.

4.5   JOB DESCRIPTION AND VARIATIONS

It is important for employers to provide a job specification for which the employee has been hired. The Employment Rights Act 1996 (s.1 ERA 1996) now requires an employer to provide a written statement of employment to the employee within two months of commencement of employment. This must include the employee's job title or a brief job description. An employee may apply to the Employment Tribunal for an order requiring the employer to provide him with a statement.

⌂   See Appendix 3 for a useful precedent of written particulars. Devising a job description will not only ensure that what is expected of the employee is clear and therefore avoid potential dispute but it may also be used to appraise the employee's performance.

Although employees are expected to have some degree of flexibility in respect of carrying out their duties, unilateral variations to an employee's job description constitute a breach of contract (*Southwark LBC* v. *Mungol* [2000] IRLB 662, EAT). Thus, employers who anticipate changes to the job description of employees should expressly reserve the power to alter any of the terms and conditions of employment.

⌂   USEFUL PRECEDENT

The Company reserves the right to vary your terms and conditions of employment in accordance with its business needs. You will be given reasonable notice prior to any changes and this will be confirmed in writing.

☞ Contractual terms may be varied in the following ways:

- verbal or written consent of the employee;
- through collective bargaining arrangements incorporated as a matter of custom and practice (*London General Transport Services Ltd* v. *Henry* [2001] IRLR 132);
- through the employee's affirmation, i.e. employee works in accordance with the new terms without objecting;
- an express clause in the contract allowing the employer to alter existing terms.

Where the employer has an express clause allowing for variations to be effected, the court expects the employer to exercise its powers in a manner that is not in breach of the relationship of trust and confidence (i.e. capriciously, without justification or exercised in a 'high handed and irresponsible manner' (*St Budeaux Royal British Legion Club* v. *Cropper* EAT 39/94)) and for the employee to be given reasonable notice of any changes (*United Bank Limited* v. *Akhtar* [1989] TRLR 507). For example, the removal of fringe benefits may not be a breach of trust and confidence whereas the suspension of substantial bonus payments generally payable to an employee who expects to receive it may undermine trust and confidence.

Variations are normally effected in writing and signed by the parties. It has however been held that it is possible for such a variation to occur by emails. So long as the person who sanctioned the variation has authority to do so, the email once printed off is deemed to be 'in writing and signed' as it bears the name of the writer (*Hall* v. *Cognos Ltd* (1998) Hull ET (1803325/97).

☞ An employer may wish to change existing contractual terms to meet changes in business needs. For example, an employee may be required to work overtime, be paid monthly rather than weekly or be subject to restrictive covenants. Variations to contractual terms are normally supported by consideration, particularly in the absence of an express clause authorising the same. Employees who are asked to consent to variations should ensure that the employer pays a price for the employee's promise (e.g. longer notice period for termination, longer annual holidays or increased salary).

⚘ If an employee refuses to consent to a proposed variation, the employer may give the employee the contractual notice to bring the existing contract to an end and offer the employee a new contract on new terms. Note however that while this will prevent a claim for wrongful dismissal, it may render the employer liable to a claim for unfair dismissal unless the employer is able to show a fair reason for the dismissal. Reorganisation of the workforce and changes to terms and conditions of employment so as to improve business efficiency (*Lesney Products and Co* v. *Nolan* [1977] IRLR 77, CA) may fall within 'some other substantial reason' (s.98(1)(b) ERA 1996) and therefore be a fair reason for dismissal.

⚘ USEFUL PRECEDENT

> *Your job description is set out in [———————]. However, the duties are not exhaustive and the Company reserves the right to ask you to undertake other duties as may from time to time be reasonably required in accordance with your capabilities and appointment.*

4.6 PLACE OF WORK

If an employee is required to work at different places, a mobility clause should be inserted in the contract to avoid any claim for breach of contract. If the employee is required to work outside Great Britain, details of the employee's allowances and currency to be paid must be stated in the written statement.

⚘ USEFUL PRECEDENT

> *Your normal place of work is [———————]. However, the Company reserves the right to require you, with reasonable notice, to work at any other establishment of the Company, whether on a temporary or permanent basis, in accordance with the Company's business needs. In the event that you have to be transferred, seconded or relocated to any other establishment of the Company, it will be carried out in accordance with the Company's relocation policy as set out in [———————].*

⚘☞ A mobility clause does not prevent a redundancy situation from arising. There can be a redundancy where there has been a reduction in the requirements of the employer's business in a location where the employee worked as a matter of fact, notwithstanding that he could be transferred to work in another establishment of the employer (*Bass Leisure* v. *Thomas* [1994] IRLR 104).

4.7   HOURS OF WORK

The Working Time Regulations 1998 ('WTR') provide that a worker may not work in excess of 48 hours a week. A worker's average weekly hours are calculated over a standard 17 weeks reference period in accordance with a formula set out in the WTR. This may be extended to 52 weeks by a collective or workforce agreement. Workers may, however, contract out of the WTR (reg. 5) but they have a right to exercise their right not to work more than 48 hours a week by giving their employer notice (such notice cannot exceed three months). Where there is a collective agreement, consent to opt out of the 48 hours a week limit must be given by individual workers, consent given by union representatives will not be sufficient (*Sindicato de Medicos de Asistencia Publica (SIMAP)* v. *Conselleria de Sanidad y Consumo de la Generalidad Valenciana* [2000] IRLR 845).

    The Horizontal Amending Directive which has to be implemented by the United Kingdom by 1 August 2003 will extend rights under the WTR to road workers, rail workers, sea workers, air workers and junior doctors. In respect of doctors, all of the WTR provisions will apply with the exception of the 48 hour week which will be phased over a period of 12 years. There is an initial four years implementation period (to commence 1 August 2004), a five year transition period (starting with a 58 hour week for the first three years and 56 hours for the next two years) with a possible extension of three years if operational difficulties are encountered. For further details, visit *www.dti.gov.uk/er/work_time_regs/exsectors.htm*

In the context of employment in the health sectors, it has recently been held by the European Court of Justice that a doctor who is 'on call' at the workplace is considered to be 'working' under the WTR. The same will not apply if the doctor who is 'on call' at home is free to undertake leisure activities at the same time (*SIMAP* v. *Conselleria de Sanidad y Consumo de la Generalidad Valenciana*).

4.8 WAGES, SALARY AND REDUNDANCY PAYMENT

The current national minimum wage for adults is £3.70 per hour and for those under 21 is £3.20 (National Minimum Wage (Increase in Development Rate for Young Workers) Regulations 2000). On 5 March 2001, the government accepted the recommendation of the independent Low Pay Commission that the adult rate should be increased to £4.10 per hour as of 1 October 2001, and £4.20 per hour as of October 2002 (see *www.dti.gov.uk/er/nmw/index.htm*).The 'youth rate' will increase to £3.50 per hour as of 1 October 2001.

An employer can only suspend an employee without pay if there is an express or implied clause in the contract authorising the employer to do so. An employee who has been laid off (s.147 ERA 1996) (where no work or pay is provided by the employer falling short of a redundancy) or put on short-time working (s.147(2) ERA 1996) (where less than half a week's pay is earned) is entitled to a guarantee payment (s.28 ERA 1996) of up to a week's pay at the statutory rate in any three month period, provided the employee has one year of continuous service prior to the workless day. If the short-time or lay off lasts for more than four consecutive weeks or six weeks in a period of 13 weeks, the employee may be able to claim a redundancy payment (s.148 ERA 1996).

If wages are due and are not paid, an employee may sue the employer for unlawful deduction of wages (s.13 ERA 1996). Wages include any fee, bonus, commission, holiday pay, statutory sick pay and statutory maternity pay. A deduction may only be deducted if a statute authorises it (e.g. an Attachment of Earnings Order is in force) or the contract expressly allows the employer to do so (e.g. the employee has taken a loan from the company, or if the employee has taken more holidays than they are entitled in any given leave year). It is lawful for an employer to claw back any 'overpayments' it has made to the employee.

Special rules on deductions apply to workers in the retail industry. This includes workers in the sale and supply of goods and financial services who may have to account for stock deficiencies or cash shortages respectively (s.17(1)–(3) ERA 1996). The employer may deduct no more than one-tenth of gross wages payable to the employee on a particular day (s.18(1) ERA 1996). Any deductions must be notified to the employee first in writing on a pay day (s.20 ERA 1996) and cannot be made after twelve months from the date when the employer first discovered or ought to have discovered the shortage or deficiency (s.18(2)(3) ERA 1996).

An employer cannot unreasonably refuse an employee the right to return to work after a period of lengthy sickness leave when the employee has been certified fit for work. At common law, an employee who offers their services is entitled to be paid unless a specific condition of the contract says otherwise (*Beveridge* v. *KLM UK Ltd* [2000] IRLR 765).

Note also that employees are entitled to equal pay for 'like work' or 'work rated as equivalent' or 'work of equal value' (Equal Pay Act 1970). To succeed, the employee has to show that a member of the opposite sex has been paid more and that an equal pay should apply.

An employee who has continuity of service with the employer for two years is entitled to a redundancy payment in the event of a redundancy (s.135 ERA 1996). An employee who leaves his employment before his employer's notice of dismissal expires may lose his right to a redundancy payment unless the employer agrees to his premature departure (s.136(3) ERA 1996).

4.9 BONUS AND STOCK OPTIONS

It should be made clear whether such entitlements are contractual or a matter of absolute discretion for the employer. If bonus payments are contractual, they should be paid net of tax as they would be deemed as 'wages'. It has been held that where the employee has a reasonable expectation to a non-contractual bonus, this will be counted as wages even in the absence of a contractual entitlement (*Kent Management Services* v. *Butterfield* [1992] ICR 272). It is submitted that this view is untenable in view of a recent decision which draws a difference between contractual and discretionary entitlements (*Cerberus Software Ltd* v. *Rowley* [2001] IRLR 160, CA) (see 5.3).

Where an annual contractual bonus is payable and the employee's contract is terminated halfway through the year, payment would be prorated (s.2 Apportionment Act 1870) on a day to day basis unless there is an express clause which provides for a different method of calculation (s.7 Apportionment Act 1870).

It has been held that where the employer has a discretionary bonus scheme (e.g. where the terms of the contract provide that '*the company may in its absolute discretion pay an annual bonus . . . the terms of any such bonus scheme to be notified to employees from time to time*') and the employee has subsequently been notified of the scheme by way of letter, the employee is entitled to the contractual bonus until such time as the scheme has been withdrawn by the employer (*Chequepoint (UK) Ltd* v. *Radwan*, IDS Brief 673).

Even where payments are subject to the discretion of the employer, it has been held that an employer exercising a discretion which on its face is unfettered or absolute will be in breach of contract, if no reasonable employer would exercise the discretion in that way (*Clark* v. *Nomura International plc* [2000] IRLR 766). An employer is required not to act 'perversely', 'irrationally' or 'capriciously' (*Manor House Healthcare* v. *Hayes* unreported, 16 October 2000, EAT 1196/99) in the exercise of its discretion. Doing so may be in breach of the implied term of trust and confidence.

⌂ Where possible avoid a contractual bonus scheme. If not, can the scheme be discretionary only? Ensure that any discretionary payment is not dependent on any factor (e.g. past performance) as this will only limit the employer's reasonable exercise of his discretion, if indeed the employee has performed well and denied payment!

☞ Employees should seek to challenge the basis upon which a discretion has been exercised by the employer in the event of non-entitlement. Where possible, compare treatment between employees as it may be possible to sustain a case for discrimination by virtue of how the employer has exercised the discretion.

4.10 HOLIDAYS

An employer is required to provide at least 20 days paid holiday to a worker who has continuous service of 13 weeks (Working Time Regulations 1998). The European Court of Justice has recently held that the 13 week requirement under the Working Time Regulations is in breach of the Working Time Directive (*R. (on the application of Broadcasting, Entertainment, Cinematographic and Theatre Union)* v. *Secretary of State for Trade and Industry (C-173/99), The Times,* 26 June 2001).

☞ Holidays continue to accrue even when an employee is off sick. An employee must be paid for any accrued holiday when the contract is terminated otherwise this may amount to an unlawful deduction of wages. Ohook what the contract says in respect of how a day's pay is to be calculated.

🔔 There is no obligation on the employer to pay the employee on public and bank holidays.

An employer may require an employee to utiltise their annual holiday at specified times, for example, during festive closures. An employee who wishes to go on holiday must provide the employer with twice the period of notice for the number of proposed holidays. The employer may refuse the request by giving as many days as possible in advance to the days it is not convenient for the employee to go on holiday (Reg. 15 Working Time Regulations 1998).

🔔 Employers should ensure that the contract provides for how accrued holiday pay is to be calculated upon termination, e.g. 1/365 of the employee's annual salary. If the contract is silent, the Apportionment Act 1870 will apply and a day's pay will be calculated by reference to a calendar day so that if an employee is entitled to 10 days' holiday, the employer will have to pay 14 days (inclusive of two weekends) (*Taylor* v. *East Midlands Offender Employment* [2000] IRLR 760). There should be an express clause disapplying the Act and to confine any accrued holiday to working days only.

4.11   SICKNESS LEAVE

It is a matter for the employer to decide if an employee should receive full contractual pay while on sick leave. An employer is not legally obliged to pay the employee the full contractual pay when they are on sick leave.

Staff absenteeism is costly for the employer. While not offering contractual sick pay may act as a deterrent against malingerers, this may also act as a disincentive on employees who are genuinely off sick. Thus, some employers offer full contractual pay for a limited period only and this may be between four and 28 weeks.

If there is no contractual sick pay, employees have a statutory right to Statutory Sick Pay (SSP) (Statutory Sick Pay (General) Regulations 1982) if their weekly earnings are within the 'lower earning limit' which is currently £66. SSP only applies to those who have been off sick for four days or more. Multiple absences of four days which are

39

not separated by a period of eight weeks may count as one qualifying period in respect of a week's sick pay. The maximum entitlement is 28 weeks in a period of three years after which the employee would have to claim Disability Benefits. The current weekly rate for SSP is £60.20 (Social Security Benefits Up-rating Order 2000).

An employee may sue the employer for an unlawful deduction of wages (s.13 ERA 1996) if the employer has failed to pay the employee SSP. As of 23 February 2001, any person who, without reasonable excuse, contravenes or fails to comply with provisions of the SSP Scheme may be guilty of an offence (s.2 Statutory Maternity Pay (General) and Statutory Sick Pay (General) (Amendments) Regulations 2001).

☞   USEFUL PRECEDENT

When your absence is due to sickness, you must:

- ensure that your manager has been notified on the first day of your absence and that your manager is personally told of the reason for absence;
- complete a self certification form on your return;
- where the absence is more than [————] days (including weekends), you must a submit a doctor's certificate to your manager and inform your manager of your likely date of return.

🔖   For more info on how to cope with staff absences, read the advisory booklet 'Absence and Labour Turnover' published by ACAS. See www.acas.org.uk.

4.12   MATERNITY LEAVE

An employee is entitled to time off for ante-natal care and has the right to be remunerated for the period of absence at the appropriate hourly rate (ss.55–56 ERA 1996).

Female employees whose Expected Week of Childbirth (EWC) begins on or after 30 April 2000 are entitled to 18 weeks of Ordinary Maternity Leave (OML), those who have one year of continuous service at the eleventh week before the EWC are entitled to a further 29 weeks of Additional Maternity Leave (AML) (The Maternity and Parental Leave etc. Regulations 1999).

OML cannot be taken earlier than 12 weeks before the expected week of childbirth. It may start at the sixth week before the expected week of childbirth or at the very latest at the date of childbirth. The 18 weeks starts to run from either one of those three periods. AML starts to run when the child is born. As a result of when AML is deemed to start, there is some overlap between OML and AML. An employee's maximum entitlement to maternity leave is therefore 40 weeks (11 weeks before childbirth and 29 weeks after childbirth) and not 47 weeks.

As with sick leave, payment during OML is a matter of contract between the employer and employee. Where there is no contractual maternity pay, employees have a statutory right to Statutory Maternity Pay (Statutory Maternity Pay (General) Regulations 1986) and the current rules on OML payment under the Scheme are:

* 90 per cent of full contractual pay for the first six weeks (higher rate);
* statutory rate for the next six weeks (lower rate);
* statutory rate for the remaining six weeks (lower rate).

The 'lower rate' is currently £60.20 but will increase to £62.20 (draft Social Security Benefits Up-rating (No. 2) Order 2000).

As of 23 February 2001, any person who, without reasonable excuse, contravenes or fails to comply with the provisions of the SMP Scheme may be guilty of an offence (s.3 Statutory Maternity Pay (General) and Statutory Sick Pay (General) (Amendment) Regulations 2001).

With effect from 17 November 2000, a female employee who qualifies for SMP but is subsequently dismissed or whose employment ended without her consent before she has started her maternity leave will remain entitled to SMP from her employer. This applies to babies born after 4 March 2001 (Statutory Maternity Pay (General) (Modification and Amendment) Regulations 2000).

☞ There is no requirement on an employer to pay an employee on Additional Maternity Leave. Employees who are only entitled to OML are presumed to be returning to work upon the expiry of the OML. For those going on to AML, the employer may not, more than 21 days before expiry of the OML, write to the employee to ask if she is returning to work after the AML. If the employee indicates that she is returning to work after the AML but changes her mind shortly before the AML expires, she would be deemed to have resigned from the job. If she has failed to provide the relevant notice period for termination, she is in breach of contract. The loss suffered by the employer may be the inconvenience in seeking a replacement at the last minute (see 6.3). An employer who decides not to offer the same job to the returning employee risks a claim for sex discrimination. To avoid this, the employer must show that there is a redundancy in the business but is still required, where possible, to offer her suitable alternative employment.

☞ An employee's contractual pay is calculated with reference to her average weekly earnings in the eight weeks up to and including the 15th week before EWC. Note complications may arise with bonuses and commissions.

An employee who does not qualify for SMP (i.e. without 26 weeks of continuous service as at the 15th week before EWC) may claim Maternity Allowance.

⚠ Employers who are arranging for temporary cover for those going on maternity leave should make it clear to prospective locums that the job is only for a specified period.

There are current proposals to increase Statutory Maternity Leave to £75 per week from April 2002 and £100 per week from April 2003 for a period of 26 weeks and a further 26 weeks unpaid maternity leave. Female employees will be entitled to a total of 52 weeks of maternity leave, bringing Britain in line with its counterparts in Europe. It is envisaged that small businesses will be able to claim some compensation for administering maternity pay from April 2002 (see www.nds.coi.gov.uk/coi/coipress.nsf).

4.13   PARENTAL LEAVE

As of 15 December 1999, employees with one year of continuous service and who have become parents are entitled to parental leave lasting 13 weeks for each child (born or adopted) up and until they reach the age of five (Maternity and Parental Leave etc. Regulations 1999), unless the child is disabled in which case the entitlement ends when the child is 18 years old. The 13 weeks entitlement is a one-off entitlement and must be carried forward from one employer to another. A female employee who has completed her maternity leave may apply for Parental Leave. The inappropriate reference to Paternity Leave is therefore misleading as a mother also has a statutory right to Parental Leave.

Employees must take Parental Leave in blocks of one week subject to a maximum of four weeks in any given year. The employees must provide the employer with at least 21 days notice before the proposed start of Parental Leave but the employer has a right to refuse the application where the employee's absence will disrupt the employer's business. In those circumstances, the employer cannot postpone the requested leave for more than six months.

⚠ There is no statutory obligation to pay anyone on Parental Leave and this is a matter of contract between the employer and employee. There are current proposals for fathers taking Parental Leave to receive Statutory Paternity Pay of £100 per week up to a maximum of two weeks as of April 2003. Parents of disabled children will be entitled to increased parental leave of 18 weeks. These proposals are expected to take effect in the later part of 2001. Visit the DTI website at *www.dti.gov.uk* for further information. See also the DTI press release (P/2001/260) published in response to the Green Paper: *Work and Parents – Competitiveness and Choice.*

On 8 May 2001, the DTI announced that Adoptive Parents Leave will be introduced by the government from 2003. Adoptive parents will be entitled to six months of paid leave at the rate of £100 per week and six months of unpaid leave. Working mothers of adopted children will therefore stand to gain £2,600. Working fathers will be entitled to two weeks paid 'paternity leave' at the rate of £100 per week. In respect of paternity leave, working fathers must provide employers with 15 weeks notice of when they intend to go on parental leave. Employers may defer the employee's request by giving four weeks' counter notice. The good news is that small employers will be able to reclaim money they pay in full plus compensation for administering adoption pay and paternity leave. (For more information see www.dti.gov.uk.)

4.14 DEPENDANT'S LEAVE

As of 15 December 1999, all employees, regardless of length of service, became entitled to reasonable time off for domestic emergencies in respect of any dependants (s.57A ERA 1996). A dependant includes a spouse, child, parent or any other person (except lodgers and tenants) who lives in the employee's household. There is no right to be paid for such time off. What is reasonable time off is a question of fact.

⌂ It was reported in the *Financial Times* in December 2000 that a woman who worked for a firm of surveyors was unfairly dismissed after she took time off to collect her sick son from school. It is automatically unfair to dismiss someone who exercises the right to Dependant's Leave.

4.15 DISCIPLINARY AND GRIEVANCE PROCEDURES

Company rules are essential to ensure that there is a level of acceptable standards in the workplace. Employees should know what is expected of them by their employers and what is considered acceptable behaviour among colleagues in the workplace. Employers are often pushed into litigation as a result of being vicariously liable for the acts of its employees who are ignorant of the employer's legal obligations. Company rules must be in place to spell out the appropriate sanctions when rules are not followed.

A disciplinary procedure enables the employer to take appropriate steps to deal with unacceptable conduct. Disciplinary action may involve a verbal warning, written warning or a dismissal in severe cases.

Whereas there is no statutory obligation for employers to have a grievance procedure, it is common to have one where the employer has a disciplinary procedure. A grievance procedure provides employees with an opportunity to raise their concerns at work with their employer including the reasonableness of any sanctions imposed by the employer. It has been held that the failure of an employer to give employees a reasonable opportunity to obtain redress of grievances is a breach of the implied term of trust and confidence (*W A Goold (Pearmak) Ltd* v. *McConnell* [1995] IRLR 516) entitling the employee to claim constructive dismissal.

Employers who wish to avoid a claim for wrongful dismissal should ensure that its disciplinary and grievance procedures are for guidance only and do not have contractual effect. If there is a contractual disciplinary and grievance procedure which has not been followed and it could be shown by the employee that it would have taken say, three months to investigate and address the alleged wrongdoing, then the employee could possibly claim three months salary for the breach of such a procedure.

⌂ As of 4 September 2000, the ACAS Code of Practice on Disciplinary and Grievance procedures came into force. These rules have 'statutory effect' in that they may be taken into account by an Employment Tribunal. Arguably, they are relevant in considering whether a dismissal has been unfair but not whether it is wrongful or otherwise. The code is relevant for the purposes of 'procedural fairness' in the context of 'misconduct dismissals' and 'incapability dismissals'.

☞ An employee has a statutory right to be accompanied by a colleague or a trade union official at a disciplinary and grievance hearing. The employee need not be party to a collective agreement. Sometimes, the contract may allow the employee to be accompanied by someone else (e.g. a friend) although this is rare in practice.

Reported cases of e-mail and internet abuse at the workplace culminating in dismissal are on the rise. Employers should have clear policies on what constitutes acceptable usage and the sanctions that would apply in the event of a breach, otherwise a dismissal for misuse (e.g. misusing passwords, installing games on company equipment or introducing a computer virus) may be deemed to be unfair (*British Telecommunications plc* v. *Rodrigues* [1995] Masons CLR Rep 93, EAT 854/92, *Gale* v. *Parknotts Ltd* 1996 Leeds ET (72487/95).

In some cases, it has been held that downloading pornography that is in violation of the employer's code of conduct (*Parr* v. *Derwentside District Council* (1998) Newcastle ET (2501507/98) or which is plainly objectionable (*Humphries* v. *V H Barnett & Co* (*a firm*) (1998) London (South) ET (2304001/97)) may amount to gross misconduct justifying summary dismissal. In other cases, it has been held that the nature of the employee's conduct was not gross enough that summary dismissal could be said to be within the range of reasonable responses open to an employer (*Dunn* v. *IBM United Kingdom Ltd* (1998) London (South) ET (2305087/97)). Current examples of conduct amounting to gross misconduct and therefore grounds for summary dismissal must be reviewed to include improper use of company's equipment. If an employer fails to take any disciplinary action on employees who download pornography which is circulated or discussed in the workplace, the employer may end up being vicariously liable for the acts of the employees which amount to sexual harassment (*Morse* v. *Future Reality Ltd* (1996) London (North) ET (54571/95)).

⚖ USEFUL PRECEDENT

The company's intranet and internet system is intended to promote business efficiency. Any misuse of the system by any employee, in the form of defamatory statements or contents constituting sexual harassment, may render the company who operates the e-mail system liable to legal action. The following rules must be observed:

- the use of inappropriate language which may be regarded as malicious, obscene or defamatory is a breach of the company's Equal Opportunities Policy and will be dealt with as a disciplinary offence;
- the deliberate or knowing misuse of the e-mail system for personal purposes constitutes gross misconduct;
- unsolicited e-mails which may contain computer viruses and pose a threat to the company's operations must not be opened but reported to the manager.

The company reserves the right to intercept any e-mail or data held on its computer files in the event that it has to monitor compliance or to investigate or detect the contravention of its e-mail policy.

Employers are now able to monitor employee e-mails without their consent if it is connected to the employer's business (Telecommunication (Lawful Business Practice) (Interceptions of Communications) Regulations 2000) without fear of breaching the employee's right to privacy under Sched. 1 Art. 8 Human Rights Act 1998. As a matter of good practice, there should still be warnings in the workplace that e-mails and voice messages may be monitored by the employer particularly when the employee is off sick.

At the time of writing, there is a draft code of practice published by the Information Commissioner governing the use of personal data in the workplace. Employers are advised to have regard to the guidelines when monitoring employees (see *www.dataprotection.gov.uk*).

4.16   NOTICE PERIOD

A contract of employment may be terminated by the employer or employee normally by giving the relevant notice for termination. An employer may agree with the employee the period of notice required for either party to terminate the contract. Longer notices of up to twelve months may apply to senior executives and directors while junior staff may be subject to a notice period of between one and three months.

In the absence of a contractual notice period, a statutory notice period will apply (s.86 ERA 1996):

- an employer must provide an employee who has worked continuously for one month but less than two months with at least one week's notice (s.86(1) ERA 1996); and then one additional week for every completed year of service subject to a maximum of twelve weeks.
- an employee need only provide the employer with one week's notice.

If there is no contractual notice period, either party may argue that there is an implied term to provide reasonable notice to terminate a contract. The fact that the employee does not have the necessary length of service to qualify for a statutory notice does not preclude a reasonable period from being implied at law (*Masiak* v. *City Restaurants (UK) Ltd* [1999] IRLR 780). The duration of a reasonable notice period would depend on the length of service, seniority, status and age of the employee. The company's financial situation is irrelevant (*Clark* v. *Fahrenheit 451 (Communications) Ltd* , IDS Brief 666, EAT).

An employee is not entitled to any notice period in the event of gross misconduct justifying summary dismissal. The employer's contract/handbook should set out a *non-exhaustive* list of examples of gross misconduct.

☞ An employee should check if the conduct complained of constitutes 'gross misconduct' in the contract. Even if the act falls within the employer's definition of gross misconduct, the employer is required to carry out a reasonable investigation before dismissing the employee summarily.

Where there is a contractual notice period for termination and the employee has failed to comply with it, any clause requiring the employee to compensate the employer (for example, by deducting a day's salary for each day when notice should have been given) must adequately reflect the employer's loss. This may be achieved by the use of a liquidated damages clause which must represent a genuine pre-estimate of the employer's loss and not a penalty clause, the latter being unenforceable (*Giraud UK Ltd* v. *Smith* [2000] IRLR 763) (see 5.1).

4.17 PAYMENT IN LIEU OF NOTICE (PILON)

If an employer wishes to be able to make a payment in lieu of notice (i.e. not require the employee to work out the notice period), this must be expressly provided for in the contract. If there is an express clause to effect a PILON, such payment would be net of tax as they would be deemed as 'wages' (*Abrahams* v. *Performing Rights Society Ltd* [1995] ICR 1028). If there is no contractual provision, any monies recovered under this head would be deemed as damages and therefore paid in gross and subject to mitigation.

If the contract provides that the employer 'may' make a payment in lieu of notice, this is not an absolute contractual right of the employee. Any monies payable by the employer in respect of the notice period will therefore be damages and subject to the employee's mitigation of loss (i.e. any earnings from the employee's new employment will be taken into account when assessing the employee's loss) (*Cerberus Software Ltd* v. *Rowley* [2001] IRLR 160, CA).

♢ Employers have to decide if:

- they want the certainty of being able contractually to require an employee not to work out the notice period when the employment relationship has broken down and compensate the employee in the form of net earnings; or
- the flexibility of a discretionary clause so that any monies payable are regarded as damages and therefore payable in gross and subject to deduction of any earnings the employee has been paid from their new employment. A discretionary clause may be a handy bargaining tool for an employer in negotiating a termination package with an employee.

4.18 RESTRICTIVE COVENANTS

It is common for employers to protect any material interest of the company by restricting the activities of its employees during employment and after the employment relationship has been terminated. This may be achieved by the use of non-competition, non-solicitation, non-dealing clauses and non-poaching covenants.

A non-competition clause seeks to prevent an employee from entering into business in competition with the employer.

A non-solicitation clause prevents the employee from approaching the clients of the employer.

A non-dealing clause prevents an employee from having any dealings with the employer's clients even when the employee is approached by them.

A non-poaching clause normally seeks to prevent the employee from taking any staff of the employer when the employee leaves the establishment.

Restrictive covenants are, on the face of it, void as they are in restraint of trade. However, these clauses are enforceable only if the scope of the restriction is no more than necessary to protect the legitimate interests of the employer (*Scully UK Ltd* v. *Lee* [1998] IRLR 259).

In this regard, the court will look at the duration of a clause, the geographical area it applies to and the nature of the clause in terms of its scope. 'Reasonable' means that it is no more than necessary to protect the employer's legitimate interest (*Wincanton Ltd* v. *Cranny* [2000] IRLR 716). A non-competition clause is more likely to be upheld if the restriction relates to an aspect of the employer's business with which the employee has been employed rather than the entire business of the employer.

A clause which deprives the employee from soliciting anyone with whom the employer or employee has had negotiations or contact with has been held to be too wide in view of the employee's influential position in the company (*International Consulting Services (UK) Ltd* v. *Hart* [2000] IRLR 227).

In respect of a non-poaching restriction, this should be confined to employees with whom the employee had personal dealings with before his termination (*TSC Europe (UK) Ltd* v. *Massey* [1999] IRLR 22, Ch D) as is the case with non-solicitation and non-dealing covenants.

Employers are naturally concerned with employees taking away with them confidential information arising from the course of employment. The court will look at the nature of the employment (i.e. the position of the employee and his exposure to confidential information) and the nature of the information (i.e. is it a trade secret such that the employee knows that it is and cannot abscond with it) (*Faccenda Chicken Limited* v. *Fowler* [1986] 3 WLR 288). Objective knowledge belongs to the employer and may be protected, but subjective knowledge belongs to the employee. An employee is allowed to go away with skills and knowledge acquired as a result of his day to day work (*FSS Travel & Leisure Systems Ltd* v. *Johnson* [1998] IRLR 382, *SBJ Stephenson Ltd* v. *Mandy* [2000] IRLR 233).

🔔 After the employment relationship has ended, only trade secrets are capable of being protected. Employers should therefore consider using an express covenant restricting the use of any information which falls short of trade secrets.

Unlike garden leave clauses (see 4.19), post-termination clauses are either enforceable or they are not as the courts do not have the power to re-write restrictive covenants. All the courts may do is sever the 'unreasonable' part of a clause provided the remaining parts still make sense after the severance (the 'blue pencil' rule). Therefore, it is not unusual to see post termination clauses drafted in the alternative so that if, say, a twelve month period is deemed too long, the employer may still fall back on the next clause covering a lesser period of, say, six months.

☞ Employees should check to see if the employer has committed a repudiatory breach of contract (e.g. has the employer been in breach of its statutory duty or the implied term of trust and confidence?). If this is the case, the employer can no longer enforce the restrictive covenants.

4.19   GARDEN LEAVE

A PILON clause merely allows an employee not to require an employee to work out the notice period. An express garden leave clause, however, goes one step further in empowering the employer to quarantine the employee for a specified time. Employees are put on garden leave where the employer's legitimate interest may be at risk. For example, the employer may not want clients to get into contact with the employee.

The purpose of a Garden Leave clause is to isolate the employee from the industry and therefore their business contacts, effectively putting the employee out of action for a certain period so that there is no risk of competition with the employer.

What constitutes reasonable time to put someone on garden leave is a question of fact. It may be between three to 12 months but all depends on the degree of the legitimate interest the employer has to protect. Unlike post-termination covenants which are either enforceable or not (i.e. the courts cannot re-write the duration of the restraints), garden leave durations may be 'whittled down' to a period deemed reasonable by the court (*Symbian Ltd v. Christensen* [2001] IRLR 77, CA).

☞ To put someone on garden leave, there must be an express provision authorising the employer to do so. There is nothing to stop an employee from working for another employer when they are not required to work out the notice period. A PILON clause may be drafted by the employer to include the right to put the employee on garden leave. In the absence of such an express provision, the employee may argue that there is an implied term that an employer has to provide a skilled employee with work if work is there to be done and the employee is willing to do it (*William Hill Organisation Ltd v. Tucker* [1998] IRLR 313). The right to work may apply to actors, piecework or commission based workers or those whose skills need constant exercise.

🔔 USEFUL PRECEDENT

When you have been given notice for termination, the company shall have the absolute right to require you not to attend work but to be placed on garden leave. During this period, you will be available during normal working hours in the event that you are required to attend work. You will continue to receive your full salary and benefits during the garden leave period but the company may in its absolute discretion:

● require you not contact, deal with or make representations to any client, customer or employee of the company without prior authority;
● require you to return all company equipment;
● require you to resign from any directorships that you hold with the Company;
● exclude you from the premises of the company or its associated offices;
● require you not to work for any other company without prior consent.

4.20   MUTUAL TRUST AND CONFIDENCE

The employer must not without reasonable and proper cause conduct themself in a manner likely to destroy or seriously damage the relationship of trust and confidence with the employee. This is an overriding obligation which is independent of and in addition to any express terms of the contract. The issue here is whether the employer has by its conduct demonstrated that it has no confidence in the employee or acted in such a manner calculated or likely to destroy or seriously damage the relationship. Examples of an employer's breach of this implied term include physical and verbal abuse (*Palmanor* v. *Cedron* [1978] IRLR 303) and bullying, unjustified criticisms and taking credit for someone else's work, failure to investigate complaints of sexual harassment (*Bracebridge Engineering Ltd* v. *Darby* [1990] IRLR 3), discrimination, unlawful demotion, requiring an employee to carry out increased duties without providing them with support (*Whitbread t/a Threshers* v. *Gullyes* 27 February 2001, CA, IDS Brief 683 April 2001), moving a senior worker to an inadequate office or location, not following an existing disciplinary procedure or imposing an unwarranted disciplinary sanction, e.g. suspending a care worker pending the outcome of an investigation into an allegation that the worker sexually abused a child in care (*Gogay* v. *Hertfordshire County Council* [2000] IRLR 703) and exercising the flexibility of an express mobility clause capriciously (*United Bank* v. *Akhtar* [1989] IRLR 507). Examples of words spoken giving rise to a breach of this implied term include: 'You can't do this bloody job anyway' (*Courtaulds Northern Textiles* v. *Andrew* [1979] IRLR 84) and 'an intolerable bitch on a Monday' (*Isle of Wight Tourist Board* v. *Coombes* [1976] IRLR 413).

An employee may also seek to argue that breach of any statutory implied term (see below) is a breach of trust and confidence.

☞   Employees who need further information on how to deal with bullying in the workplace should access www.successunlimited.co.uk/.

Note that an employee may be in breach of trust and confidence by disclosing confidential information to third parties (*Winder* v. *The Commissioner of Inland Revenue* (1998) Ashford ET (1101770/97) or misusing company equipment (*Parr* v. *Derwentside District Council* (1998) Newcastle ET (2501507/98).

The implied term of trust and confidence does not require either the employer or employee to disclose any wrongdoing (*Bank of Credit and Commerce International SA* v. *Ali* [1999] ICR 1068, Ch D). Neither party is required to disclose facts material to the decision of the other party whether to enter into a contract (*Bell* v. *Lever Brothers* [1932] AC 161, HL) or whether exercising a certain option would be less advantageous financially to the employee (*University of Nottingham* v. *Eyett* (No. 1) [1999] 2 All ER 437, Ch D).

4.21   GOOD FAITH AND FIDELITY

An employee is required not to act in a manner which will seriously harm the employer's business. This includes not carrying on business in competition with the employer, using the employer's list of customers, information on their business needs, confidential information and trade secrets. Conversely, the employer cannot disclose information about an employee to a third party without good reason or consent (see 4.23 on the Data Protection Act 1998).

The implied duty of fidelity applies so long as the employment relationship subsists (*Hivac Ltd* v. *Park Royal Scientific Instruments Ltd* [1946] 1 All ER 350). Despite a recent High Court decision (*Symbian Ltd* v. *Christensen* [2001] IRLR 77) which held that the operation of a garden leave clause destroys an employment relationship so that an employee is no longer under an implied duty of fidelity (and thus, arguably the employee is able to plot against his employer), the better view is that the duty of fidelity still applies even when an employee has been sent on garden leave. The judge who held that the 'contractual relationship' still subsists but not the 'employment relationship' when the employee is on garden leave does not sit well with employment lawyers and it has been argued that the case ought to be confined to its own facts.

⌂   Include an express provision that the implied term of fidelity (e.g. not to compete with the employer) shall continue during the 'contractual term' even when the employee is on garden leave

⌂   Ensure that all company equipment and property including laptops, mobile telephones and customer information are duly returned to the employer when the employee is placed on garden leave.

☞ In respect of what is knowledge capable of protection by the employer, it has been held that *objective* knowledge belongs to the employer whereas *subjective* knowledge belongs to the employee which may be taken away after the employment relationship has ended (*SBJ Stephenson Ltd* v. *Mandy* [2000] IRLR 233).

4.22 REFERENCES

Although an employer is under an implied duty to act in good faith towards the employee, such duty ceases when the employment relationship comes to an end.

An employer is under no statutory obligation to provide a reference in respect of a former employee (but see *Coote* v. *Granada Hospitality Ltd* [1998] IRLR 656, in the context of victimisation under the Sex Discrimination Act 1975).

It has always been thought that there is no common law obligation to provide a reference after the employment relationship has ended but it has been held that, in certain circumstances, there may be an implied obligation to provide one, e.g. where the person requesting it is a regulatory body such as the Financial Services Authority (*Spring* v. *Guardian Assurance* [1994] IRLR 460, HL).

Where an employer decides to provide a reference during the period of the employment contract, it has been held that there is a contractual obligation on the part of the employer to prepare it with reasonable skill and care (*TSB Bank plc* v. *Harris* [2000] IRLR 157).

If an employer is minded to provide a reference, it also owes a duty of care to a third party (the former employee's prospective employer) so that the contents must be fair, accurate, reasonable and not misleading (*Kidd* v. *Axa Equity & Law Life Assurance Society plc* [2000] IRLR 301). Even if the contents of the reference are factual, it must not be selective so that an overall detrimental picture is painted of the employee. It has been held that there is no legal obligation to provide a full and comprehensive reference. If the reference is inaccurate or misleading, the employer may be liable for negligent mis-statement (*Spring* v. *Guardian Assurance*), tort of deceit, malicious falsehood and defamation. In a recent case, an employer who mentioned in a reference that complaints had been made against the former employee even though the former employee had been unaware of the complaints, was found to be negligent (*TSD Bank plc v Harris*).

☞ Current discrimination laws only apply to discriminatory acts during employment (*Adekeye v. Post Office (No. 2)* [1997] IRLR 105, *Relaxion Group plc v. Rhys-Harper* [2001] IRLR 810, EAT). However, an employee who has instituted discrimination proceedings against the employer and is victimised after the employment relationship has ended (e.g. if they receive an adverse reference after termination of employment) may be able to sue the employer for victimisation even if the act complained of is after termination of employment (*Coote v. Granada Hospitality Ltd* [1998] IRLR 656).

● Ensure that offers made to prospective employees are subject to receipt of satisfactory references in writing. In your request for a reference, focus on factual questions and probe key issues relating to the job advertised. Expressly reserve the right to terminate the employment if unsatisfactory references have been received (see 4.3).

Δ Guidelines for references:

● If you are minded to provide a reference, ensure that it is consistent with the reason for dismissal or reason for leaving. A 'good' reference may be used against an employer who has dismissed an employee for misconduct or incompetence. The reference must also mirror the employee's written reasons for dismissal which employees are entitled to if they have continuity of service of one year with the employer.

● Ensure that any information provided in a reference does not breach the Data Protection Act 1998. For example, where there is sensitive data relating to the employee's sickness records, you need to obtain permission from the employee first. The employee does not have a right to see a copy of the reference (Sched. 7 Data Protection Act 1998) although they may request to see a copy from the prospective employer. Employers acting as public authorities should ensure that there is no breach of Sched. 1 art. 8 Human Rights Act 1998 (right to respect for private and family life) if a reference contains intimate details of the employee.

● Keep any reference factual to avoid any liability for negligent mis-statement. Otherwise, decline the request for a reference. The employer may however be required to provide an agreed reference as part of any settlement negotiated where the employee has issued proceedings against the employer. Again, keep it factual.

☞ Although an employee does not have a general legal right to insist on being provided with a reference from the former employer, they may be able to obtain one as part of any proposals for settlement out of court.

⌂ For more info on references, visit the Chartered Institute of Personnel and Development website: www.ipd.co.uk/Infosource/ LegalIssues/References.asp.

4.23   STATUTORY IMPLIED TERMS

An employee may seek to argue that an employer's breach of a statutory term is a breach of the term of trust and confidence. Breach of any statutory implied term may entitle an employee to resign and sue for constructive wrongful dismissal. But breach of statutory implied terms have greater ramifications for the employer as the employee may resign and claim constructive unfair dismissal following an assertion of their statutory rights (s.104(1) ERA 1996; these include rights under the ERA, Working Time Regulations 1998 and those under the Trade Union Labour Relations (Consolidation) Act 1992). A dismissal of an employee who has exercised their statutory rights is automatically unfair and no qualifying period is necessary. Employers should watch out for a potential claim of unfair and wrongful dismissal.

Sex Discrimination Act 1975, Equal Pay Act 1970, Race Relations Act 1976 and Disability Discrimination Act 1995

An employee and job applicant has a statutory right not to be treated less favourably by reason of their sex, pregnancy, marriage, gender re-assignment, race and/or disability. The SDA and RRA prohibit direct and indirect discrimination whereas the DDA only applies to direct discrimination.

☞ Employees who have been treated less favourably as a result of exercising their rights under the SDA, RRA and DDA or having done a 'protected act' under the SDA and RRA may sue for victimisation. A 'protected act' includes speaking up for the rights of others or testifying against the employer.

Direct discrimination occurs when the employer treats the employee less favourably by reason of their gender, gender re-assignment, race (discrimination on the ground of colour, race or ethnic or national origins is prohibited) or disability Examples of direct discrimination include:

- an employer's refusal to hire someone who has undergone a sex operation even though the person is capable of performing the job advertised;

- an employer's refusal to employ someone or decision to dismiss someone who is of the opposite sex (*Moran* v. *RBR International Ltd* ET/2302446/00), married (*Cave* v. *Ripon Cathedral Choir School Ltd* ET/1805999/00), pregnant or who has children (*Wickramaratne* v. *Wellington Estate Agents (Battersea) Ltd* ET 2304283/00);

- an employer's refusal to hire someone or decision to dismiss someone who is not of British nationality or who is of ethnic minority origins (*Benjamin & Costa* v. *JD Wetherspoon Plc* ET 2200975/00);

- an employer's refusal to hire an English person in preference for a Scot (*BBC Scotland* v. *Souster* [2001] IRLR 150) – there can be discrimination between the English, Welsh, Scots and Irish as they are of different *national origins* although they may be of the same nationality.

It has recently been held by the Court of Session that the word 'sex' under the Sex Discrimination Act only applies to 'gender' and does not include sexual orientation (*Secretary of State for Defence* v. *MacDonald* [2001] IRLR 431, CS). The Court overruled the decision of the Scottish EAT in *MacDonald* v. *Ministry of Defence* [2000] IRLR 748 and followed the English EAT's devision in *Pearce* v. *Governing Body of Mayfield Secondary School* [2000] IRLR 548.

There is no defence of justification for direct discrimination unless the employer is able to show cause for positive action or a genuine occupational qualification defence applies (see below). The issue is whether the person allegedly discriminated against would have been treated differently but for their sex, race or disability. The motives, prejudices and intentions of the discriminator are irrelevant.

The onus of proof is on the person alleging discrimination but when the EU Burden of Proof Directive (Council Directive 97/80/EC) comes into force on 22 July 2001, an Employment Tribunal will be required to draw an inference of discrimination where the employer has failed to rebut evidence of facts which gives rise to a presumption of direct discrimination.

* Employees should try and prove less favourable treatment by way of an actual comparator, if not, a hypothetical comparator. Use statistics across the employer's workforce to show differential treatment by the employer.

Indirect discrimination occurs when the employer imposes a requirement or condition such that the proportion of people sharing the same sex or race of the employee being able to comply with the requirement or condition is considerably smaller than those who do not share the same attributes as the person discriminated against. Examples of indirect discrimination include conditions imposed in respect of the following:

- qualifications, experience and languages;
- length of service;
- height;
- dress sense;
- mobility;
- shift patterns.

In respect of sex and race discrimination, the employer may rely on a defence of 'genuine occupational qualification' (s.7 Sex Discrimination Act 1975 and s.5 Race Relations Act 1976) or 'positive action' (s.7(2)(e) Sex Discrimination Act 1975 and s.5(2)(d) Race Relations Act 1976). The GOQ defence may include reasons connected to the physiology or authenticity of a person (e.g. an actor, entertainer, model or the running of a restaurant) or where the employer has to provide personal services to people of the same sex or race. Positive action will include the provision of personal services and encouraging applications from members of a particular sex/race.

Employees and job applicants who suffer from a disability may be protected under the DDA 1995. Disability is defined as 'a physical or mental impairment which has a substantial and long term adverse effect on a person's ability to carry out normal day to day activities'. Sufferers of hayfever, kleptomania, alcoholism are not 'disabled' whereas dyslexia is a recognised disability (*Banyard* v. *Prudential Assurance Co. Ltd* (2000) EAT 1431/99 IDS Brief 682, April 2001).

Those who suffer from a progressive condition such as cancer, multiple sclerosis and HIV infection will be considered 'disabled' once the condition manifests itself and is likely to result in impairment which has a substantial adverse effect. When assessing whether a condition has a substantial adverse effect on the employee, the Tribunal must focus on what the employee is unable to do rather than what they can do (*Leonard* v. *Southern Derbyshire Chamber of Commerce* [2001] IRLR 19, EAT) including the effect of medication (*Goodwin* v. *Patent Office* [1999] IRLR 4). The role of experts is to provide an opinion on the complainant's prognosis and the effect of medication, not to draw legal conclusions as to whether the complainant's impairment is substantial (*Vicary* v. *British Telecommunications plc* [1999] IRLR 680). The EAT has emphasised that it is for the Tribunal and not the medical experts to decide whether the medical condition of the complainant falls within the definition of 'disability' (*Abadeh* v. *British Telecommunications plc* [2001] IRLR 23).

Disability discrimination is prohibited in two ways:

(i) less favourable treatment by reason of the employee's disability (s.5(1) DDA 1995);

(ii) failure to make reasonable adjustments (s.5(2) DDA 1995);

unless the employer can show that the discriminatory treatment is justified in that it is substantial and material to the circumstances of the particular case (*Fu* v. *Camden LBC* [2001] IRLR 186, EAT). There is no equivalent of a 'GOQ' or 'positive action' defence as is the case with sex and race discrimination. It has been held by the Court of Appeal that the defence of justification (in particular, the interpretation of the word 'substantial', i.e the credibility of the employer's decision) must be considered with reference to the 'band of reasonable responses test' applied in unfair dismissal cases (*Jones* v. *Post Office* [2001] EWCA Civ 558, *Foley* v. *Post Office* [2000] IRLR 827).

In respect of less favourable treatment, the comparator is someone who does not suffer from the disability of the employee. There is no need for 'like for like' comparison, i.e. an employee who has been off sick due to his disability need not compare himself with someone who has been off sick for other reasons but for a disability. The Tribunal will look at whether the reason for the less favourable treatment is for a disability reason, which does not apply to other employees (*Clark* v. *Novacold Ltd* [1999] IRLR 318, CA, *British Sugar plc* v. *Kirker* [1998] IRLR 624, EAT).

Where there is a duty to make adjustments, less favourable treatment cannot be justified unless it can be shown that the treatment would have been justified even after making the adjustments.

Discriminatory treatment may be justified and so is the employer's failure to make reasonable adjustments. The court will draw a balance between the interests of the employer and those of the employee (the 'cost/benefit' basis). Reasonable adjustments include interview and selection procedures, job offers, modifications to premises (e.g. access to the building, toilet facilities and lighting), equipment (e.g. adapted keyboard and large print), hours of work, training, supervision, and time off for care. The employer may not be required to make adjustments where it is impractical, ineffective or to do so will result in financial hardship and disruption to the employer (see Code of Practice for the Elimination of Discrimination in the Field of Employment Against Disabled Persons).

☞ An employer is only required to make reasonable adjustments if it is aware, or has reasonable grounds to be aware, of the employee's disability (s.6(6) DDA 1995). However, this is an objective test which places the burden of enquiry on the employer (*HJ Heinz Co Ltd* v. *Kenrick* [2000] IRLR 144, EAT).

☞ Recent case law suggest that sexuality discrimination is not covered under the Sex Discrimination Act. Now that the Human Rights Act 1998 is in place, an employee of a public authority may however seek to rely on a right to privacy and family life if they are discriminated against on grounds of sexuality at the workplace (Sched. 1 art. 8 Human Rights Act 1998). A new Employment Framework Directive now requires all member states in the European Union to enact domestic legislation to curb discrimination on grounds of sexual orientation and religion by 2003, and age and disability discrimination by 2 December 2006.

☞ An employee is under no statutory obligation to disclose any disability to the employer. Where the employer requires the employee to declare if the employee has any illness and the employee fails to disclose it at the time of the job offer, the employer may subsequently dismiss the employee for deceit (probably under the 'some other substantial reason' head). However, such a dismissal may be unfair as it may constitute disability discrimination. Employers should consider if the illness of the employee is likely to affect the employee's performance including any risk to health and safety.

☞ Note that the government has proposed to extend the DDA 1995 to apply to employers with fewer than 15 employees by October 2004.

Employees with cancer or who are registered partially sighted will be deemed as disabled within the legal meaning of disability.

Health and Safety at Work Act 1974 ('HASAWA'), Workplace (Health, Safety and Welfare) Regulations 1992 ('WR'), Management of Health and Safety at Work Regulations 1999 ('MHSAW')

An employer is under a common law duty to ensure the health and safety of its workforce (*Johnstone* v. *Bloomsbury Health Authority* [1991] 2 All ER 293). Under the HSAWA 1974 (s.2(1)), the employer has to ensure so far as is reasonably practicable, the health, safety and welfare of its employees and others sharing the workplace. This duty extends to systems of work, working practices and procedures, machinery and plant and the working environment.

The Health and Safety Executive and local authorities are responsible for enforcing the HASAWA 1974 and all relevant statutory provisions. An inspector has the power to serve an Improvement Notice (requiring the employer to remedy a breach) or a Prohibition Notice (directing the employer not to carry out certain activities involving potential risk of serious injury).

If work equipment is defective, the employee may sue the employer under the Employers' Liability (Defective Equipment) Act 1969 if fault is attributable to a third party, e.g. the manufacturer. Employers are now required to provide employees with safe work equipment and safe usage by way of appropriate training under the Provision and Use of Work Equipment Regulations 1998. The Personal Protective Equipment at Work Regulations 1992 require an employer to provide employees with suitable equipment to include work clothing/gear without charge to the employee.

The WR 1992 require the employer to address specific issues to ensure that the workplace is safe including ventilation and temperature of indoor work areas, lighting, floor area, height and occupied space, adequacy of work stations, seating arrangements, accommodation and rest rooms.

The Health and Safety (Display Screen Equipment) Regulations 1992 impose an obligation on employers to ensure that those working with VDUs are subject to risks assessment. These include regular eye tests, provision of corrective equipment and rest breaks.

The Reporting of Injuries, Diseases and Dangerous Occurrences Regulations 1995 require an employer to report work related accidents to the local authority as soon as practicable. An accident resulting in the incapacitation of an employee for more than three days must be reported within 10 days. For an accident report form, see www. riddor.gov.uk .

The MHSAW Regulations 1999 re-enact the 1992 regulations and require employers to carry out a hazard study or risk assessment of the workplace and to adopt preventative measures in respect of the employees' safety (regs. 3 and 4 Management of Health and Safety at Work Regulations 1992). These obligations include risks assessments and avoidance, the appointment of a health and safety representative and the availability of first aid and emergency services in the event of an accident. Breach of these statutory duties is a criminal offence punishable with a fine and/or imprisonment. The employer may also be liable in the tort of negligence.

Despite these obligations imposed on the employer, the employee is under a duty to inform the employer of any danger to their health and safety and to exercise reasonable care in respect of their persons as well as their colleagues.

Bullying claims and stress claims caused by increased workload (*Walker* v. *Northumberland County Council* [1995] IRLR 35: Mr Walker was awarded £175,000 in damages, *Jones* v. *Sandwell MBC* unreported, 31 October 2000, Birmingham County Court: Mr Jones was awarded £157,541 in damages for stress due to bullying, harassment and excessive workload) have become quite common in recent years. Where work-related stress is not addressed, the employee may resign and claim constructive dismissal (*Isle of Wight Tourist Board* v. *Coombes* [1976] IRLR 413).

△ Employers should:

- carry out risk assessments and conduct stress surveys;
- establish a clear policy on mental health and stress and offer counselling where applicable;
- establish an anti-bullying or harassment policy in the workplace;
- warn employees that bullying constitutes gross misconduct justifying dismissal;
- appraise employees' work regularly;

- encourage use of the company's grievance procedure;
- provide training for those employees who are new or those whose job responsibilities have changed;
- minimise pressure on employees.

☞ Employees are able to sue the employer for physical or mental injury provided that the injury is foreseeable to the employer. In considering whether the damage is foreseeable, the court will take into account whether the employee had alerted the employer of the problem or has taken time off work for stress. The employer's duty of care is to protect employees from reasonably foreseeable physical and psychiatric harm but not mere unpleasant emotions such as grief, anger, resentment and normal human conditions such as anxiety and stress (*Fraser v. State Hospitals Board for Scotland* (2000) Rep LR 94).

Transfer of Undertakings (Protection of Employment) Regulations 1981 ('TUPE')

The Transfer of Undertakings (Protection of Employment) Regulations 1981 (reg. 5(5) TUPE 1981) are designed to protect employees both before and after a business has been acquired by another company or where two companies merge. Whether there is a 'relevant transfer' within the meaning of the Regulations depends on a host of factors which cannot be considered in isolation (*Cheeseman and others v. R. Brewer Contracts Ltd* [2001] IRLR 144). They include:

- is there a stable, discrete and identifiable economic entity which is capable of being transferred?
- has the entity retained its identity after the transfer?
- have assets transferred?
- in the case of labour intensive businesses, has there been a transfer of a majority of the workforce? If not, why not?
- the absence of a contractual relationship between the seller and purchaser does not preclude a transfer.

A seller company (transferor) or a purchaser company (transferee) cannot change the existing contractual terms of an employee if that will result in a substantial detriment to the employee. There is nothing to prevent a purchaser from offering more attractive terms to the employees to maintain the employees of the seller after the transfer.

Employers may wish to harmonise the terms and conditions of their staff following a transfer. Harmonisation is part of good industrial practice to ensure uniformity and fairness in the workplace. This is, however, not possible if such variation is said to be 'connected' to the transfer. It has been held that a mere lapse of time of up to two years without a separate intervening act between the transfer and any subsequent variations to the terms and conditions of employees will not break the causal link so that the variation is lawful (*Taylor* v. *Connex South Eastern Ltd* unreported, 5 July 2000, IDS Brief 670, EAT).

Where the employee has been dismissed for an 'economic, technical and organisational (ETO) reason' by the transferor and re-employed by the transferee on new terms, this is not a reason connected with the transfer so that the variation is a breach of the Regulations (*Wilson* v. *St Helens BC* [1999] 2 AC 52). Whereas dismissal for an ETO reason may be a fair reason under the head of 'some other substantial reason', the employer is still required to act fairly in bringing about the dismissal.

⌂ An employee may object to a transfer (reg. 5(4A) TUPE 1981); however, they would be deemed to have resigned and not dismissed (reg. 5(4B) TUPE 1981).

☞ The employee may have a constructive wrongful and unfair dismissal claim if the resignation, before or after the transfer, amounts to a constructive dismissal arising from a threat or proposal to vary to the employees' contractual terms which involves a substantial and detrimental change to their working conditions (*Oxford University* v. *Humphreys* [2000] IRLR 183). The employee need not show that the employer's conduct amounts to a repudiatory breach of contract in order to prove constructive dismissal in the context of a transfer of undertakings (*Rossiter* v. *Pendragon plc* [2001] IRLR 256, EAT).

⌂ Regulation 12 of TUPE provides that it is not possible for an employee to contract out of their rights under the Regulations. Section 203 ERA 1996, however, provides that an employee may contract out of their rights to sue for unfair dismissal in the form of a Compromise Agreement. Arguably, it is possible to circumvent the Regulations if the employee is prepared to waive their rights to sue for unfair dismissal even if the reason for dismissal is connected to TUPE.

The Contracts (Rights of Third Parties) Act 1999 came into force on 11 May 2000. The Act provides that a third party, who is not privy to a contract, may nonetheless enforce a term of the contract where that term seeks to confer a benefit on that third party. The third party is not required to provide any consideration to enforce the contract. Where a transferor and transferee provide for certain benefits in a business acquisition agreement which is outside the existing terms of the employee's contract (e.g. more holiday entitlement, a contractual redundancy scheme and pension scheme), the employee may be able to enforce these benefits under the Act provided that the contract is enforceable between the contracting parties.

Employment Rights Act 1996

An employee has a statutory right:

- to a written statement of employment (s.1 ERA 1996);
- not to be unfairly dismissed (s.94 ERA 1996);
- to a written statement for dismissal after one year of service (s.92 ERA 1996); unless the reason for dismissal is automatically unfair in which case no qualifying period is necessary;
- not to have unlawful deduction of wages made (s.13 ERA 1996);
- to statutory minimum notice of termination in the absence of a contractual notice (s.87 ERA 1996);
- not to be laid off without a guarantee payment (s.28 ERA 1996);
- to a redundancy payment (s.135 ERA 1996);
- to time off for public duties (s.50 ERA 1996);
- to time off to look for alternative employment if made redundant (s.52 ERA 1996);
- to time off to take part in trade union activities or as an employee representative (s.61 ERA 1996);
- to time of for ante-natal care (s.55 ERA 1996);
- to accompany a worker or be accompanied by a worker/union official at a disciplinary and grievance hearing (ss.10–15 Employment Relations Act 1999);
- to reasonable time off for dependants (ss.57A and 57B ERA 1996).

☞ An employee who works under a fixed term contract may be deprived of a right to claim a redundancy payment if the contract is not renewed (s.197(3) ERA 1996) but the employee cannot be made to give up their right to claim unfair dismissal (s.197(1) ERA 1996 repealed by s.18(1) Employment Relations Act 1999) unless this is enshrined in a valid Compromise Agreement (see 8.5).

Public Interest Disclosure Act 1998

Employees are protected from dismissal or from suffering a detriment if they disclose certain wrongdoing by their employer. This protection came into force on 2 July 1999. The Act provides that an employee is protected from whistleblowing if they make a 'qualifying disclosure' and have followed the correct disclosure procedure but are dismissed or made to suffer a detriment as a result of the disclosure (s.47B ERA 1996).

The employee may raise the alarm if the employer has:

- committed a criminal wrong;
- failed to comply with a legal obligation;
- committed a miscarriage of justice;
- endangered health and safety;
- endangered the environment.

or information relating to the above is likely to be concealed.

The Act promotes an internal disclosure within the company (e.g. disclosure to the employee's line manager at first instance) failing which external disclosure to the relevant authorities may be made. An employee has to make a disclosure in good faith. If there is a breach of the Act, damages are unlimited.

Cases brought under the Act have involved pornography in the workplace (*Chattenton* v. *City of Sunderland City Council* ET 6402938/99), standards of patient care in nursing homes (*Blandon* v. *ALM Medical Services Ltd* ET 2405845/99), and a director making bogus expenses claims (*Fernandes* v. *Netcom Consultants (UK) Ltd* ET 2200060/00).

△ Employers may seek to argue that the reason for the employee's dismissal was not connected to a protected disclosure but for another reason, e.g. redundancy.

☞ Employees are generally reluctant to testify against their employer in Employment Tribunal proceedings on behalf of their colleagues for fear of repercussions in the workplace. However, the PIDA is designed to protect employees from suffering a detriment falling short of dismissal and dismissal itself.

Human Rights Act 1998

The HRA 1998 came into force on 2 October 2000. Employees whose rights are infringed under the Act no longer need to seek redress in the European Court of Human Rights as the UK courts now have jurisdiction to hear these complaints.

It has been argued that the Act is directly enforceable against public authorities and those with mixed private and public functions (i.e. it has vertical effect) but not against private companies or between private individuals (i.e. horizontal effect) (see *The Impact of the Human Rights Act on Private Law: the Knight's Move* (2000) 116 LQR 380 and compare *Horizons of Horizontality* (2000) 116 LQR 217; *De Keyser Ltd* v. *Wilson* [2001] IRLR 324, EAT: Lindsay P seems to have endorsed the view that the Act only has vertical effect).

The Act does not create a free standing right for employees in both the public and private sectors. There is no statutory obligation on an employer to guarantee employees the right, for example, to a private life, family life, the freedom of expression, thought, conscience and religion.

However, public sector employees may be able to argue that certain aspects of the employment relationship breach the provisions of the Act. Private sector employees who are unable to rely on the Act directly would have to rely on the court's intervention indirectly to enforce their rights. A tribunal or court of law is a public authority and will have to ensure, when adjudicating employment disputes, that employers have not behaved in a manner in the employment relationship that is inconsistent with the employee's rights under the Act (s.6 Human Rights Act 1998).

If the UK adopts the Charter of Fundamental Rights in the future, this will take the Act further in that no distinction will be made between public and private employees.

The rights under the Act are set out in Sched. 1 HRA 1998 and these mirror the Articles set out in the European Convention on Human Rights. Most of the rights are not absolute rights but may be limited by the employer if any interference with the employee's rights is justified. Here are some of the salient points:

Article 3: freedom from torture, inhuman or degrading treatment or punishment

An employee may argue that long periods of suspension from work pending the outcome of a disciplinary investigation is a breach. Long hours of work are unlikely to be a breach as the worker has the option of resigning from the employer.

Article 6: Right to a fair hearing within a reasonable time by an independent and impartial tribunal established by law in the determination of his/her civil rights and obligations

This is unlikely to apply to internal disciplinary hearings as they do not constitute the determination of the employee's 'civil rights'. There is a right to a *public* hearing so that rooms allocated for a tribunal hearing must be accessible to the public (*Storer* v. *British Gas plc*, IDS Brief 659).

Article 8: Right to respect for private and family life.

An employer's use of over intrusive policies such as video surveillance and monitoring of employee's communications may amount to a breach (*Halford* v. *United Kingdom* [1997] IRLR 471). The employer will have to justify the restriction as being necessary to ensure security, avoiding legal liability or maintaining the company's image (Art. 8 (2) ECHR). If employees' consumption of alcohol has to be monitored for health and safety reasons by way of breathalyser tests, this should be made known to employees in advance. Misuse of alcohol should be made a disciplinary offence justifying dismissal. Sexual orientation discrimination in the workplace may be challenged as unlawful (*Lustig-Prean and Beckett* v. *United Kingdom* [1999] IRLR 734). Employers may have to draw a balance between work life and family commitment of employees. Family friendly policies in the form of the Working Time Regulations 1998, Parental Leave and Adoption Leave have recently been introduced by the government.

⌂ Substance abuse by employees may be a conduct issue but equally become a medical issue. If the problem is a medical one, the employer should be mindful of the DDA 1995. An employer should have a clear written policy on screening for alcohol and drug abuse and spell out to employees the implications of testing positive. In this way, the employer's screening policy is more unlikely to fall foul of Art. 8 but deemed as lawful and proportionate.

Article 9: Freedom of thought, conscience, religion

Employees may seek to argue that they have the right to religious belief and therefore time off to attend religious ceremonies (*Ahmad* v. *UK* (1982) 4 EHRR 126). While the right to hold beliefs is absolute, the right to manifest them is subject to limitation necessary in a democratic society. So if an employer insists that an employee should give up their belief or face dismissal (*Knudsen* v. *Norway* (1985) 42 DR 247), this is a breach of Art. 9 but there is no breach where an employee refuses to sign a contract which contained terms requiring them to work on Sundays which is against the employee's religious commitments (*Stedman* v. *UK* (1997) 23 EHHR CD 168).

Article 10: Freedom of expression

Employees may argue that they have the right to dress in whatever they choose. Employers may, however, limit such freedom for health and safety reasons and to protect the business's image (*Kara* v. *United Kingdom* [1999] EHRLR 232). However, dress-down days are now becoming increasingly common even with corporate giants. In respect of freedom of speech, the position is governed by the Public Interest Disclosure Act 1998 but an employee may argue that they have a right to make a non 'protected disclosure'. If an employer uses a 'gagging clause' to restrict an employee from disclosing non-confidential information or from making disparaging remarks after the employment has ended, such a clause will have to be justified. The use of confidentiality clauses by employers may also be affected by Art. 10.

Article 11: Freedom of association and assembly

Employees may have a collective (not individual) right to join a trade union but there is no automatic right to strike. The position governing trade union recognition is enshrined in s.1 Employment Relations Act 1999 (inserting a new Sched. A1 Trade Union and Labour Relations (Consolidation) Act 1992). It is arguable that the six-picket rule which applies to industrial action but not to other public demonstrations may be a breach of this article. Similarly, a restriction on where a picket may be held could constitute a breach.

Article 14: Prohibition against discrimination

This Article provides that the enjoyment of rights under the Act shall be secured without discrimination on any grounds. However, this is not a free standing right to freedom from discrimination but limited to the right to enjoy any of the rights without discrimination.

☞ Breach of any of the rights under the Act may be deemed as the breach of the implied term of trust and confidence between the employer and employee. However, many of the rights under the Act may be limited if the interference is legitimate, relevant, proportionate and necessary in a democratic society.

In what has been described as the first employment law decision on the application of the Act (*De Keyser* v. *Wilson* [2001] IRLR 324, EAT), the EAT held that the employer's provision of sensitive information relating to the employee's personal problems to a joint expert (in that case, an occupational health specialist) for the preparation of a report to be used by the parties in a stress claim did not infringe Art. 6 or 8 of the Act. The EAT held that the employee's right to privacy had to be qualified only so far as 'necessary . . . for the protection of the rights and freedoms of others' (Art. 8(2) ECHR) — in that case, by the right to both parties to have a fair trial bearing in mind that the employee instituted the proceedings.

Cases from the European Court of Human Rights confirm that the rights under the Act may be limited by contract provided such waiver is clear and certain to both parties (*Ahmad* v. *UK* (1982) 4 EHRR 126).

For further information on human rights issues, see www.homeoffice.gov.uk/hract/hrafags.htm, www.beagle.org.uk/hra/newindex.htm, www.echr.coe.int/

Data Protection Act 1998

The above Act came into force on 1 March 2000 as a result of the recognition that an individual should be aware of, and have some degree of control over, the nature of data held on their behalf by a data processor. An employer is a data processor if they obtain, store, record, disclose or transmit any information in relation to the employee. The Act (s.55 Data Protection Act 1998) prohibits the unlawful obtaining or disclosing of personal data by those who have access to the employee's personal data. This includes both the employer and their fellow workers. It is an offence knowingly to disclose, or recklessly obtain, personal data without the consent of the employee concerned, unless this was necessary to prevent or detect a crime, the disclosing employee had the legal right to do so or it was in the public interest.

The Act restricts employers processing 'sensitive personal data' without the explicit consent of the employee. This includes racial origin, political opinions, membership of trade union, physical or mental health, sexual life and criminal history. Employers are, however, allowed to process sensitive personal data in order to perform a legal obligation (e.g. recording details of the employee's sickness record for sick pay purposes, to monitor equal opportunities in the workplace (e.g. asking employees to indicate their racial or ethnic background), to carry out a trade union's legitimate interest, or processing is in the substantial public interest (e.g. the employee's malpractice or incompetence).

Employers are advised to keep as little sensitive personal data as possible. If information has come to the employer's attention, is it necessary for it to be recorded? (e.g. details of whether an employee is HIV or has a criminal record). If this is necessary because of the nature of the employee's job, the employer should ensure it obtains consent from the employee first.

The Data Protection Commissioner (known as the Information Commissioner as of 30 January 2001) has powers to refrain employers from processing certain data or to destroy or erase inaccurate data. Warrants may be issued to allow entry on to premises and the inspection of data. Where an employee has suffered losses as a result of the employer's failure to comply with the Act, damages may be awarded. An employee may suffer a loss if inaccurate data held leads to a dismissal, if false information has been put in a reference or inaccurate information causes an employee to lose out on promotion or other opportunities. Such disputes are heard by the Information Tribunal.

For further information, see www.dataprotection.gov.uk.

Part Time Workers (Prevention of Less Favourable Treatment) Regulations 2000

The above legislation came into force on 1 July 2000. The Regulations make it unlawful for employers to treat part timers less favourably in their terms and conditions than full timers. Part timers should

- receive the same hourly rate as comparable full timers;
- receive the same hourly rate of overtime once they have worked more than the normal full time hours of full timers;
- not be excluded from training because they are part timers;
- have the same entitlements to annual leave and parental/maternity leave on a pro-rata basis as full timers.

The Regulations apply to employees and workers. However, part timers may only compare themselves with full timers on similar contracts working for the same company. Where there is no full time comparator in the same establishment, the part timer may compare themselves with a full timer engaged in similar work in a different establishment of the employer. Part timers who were once full timers may compare their terms with their previous contracts to ensure that there is no less favourable treatment. Employees have a right to a written statement of reasons from the employer within 21 days if they suspect that there is unfavourable treatment. Small businesses are not exempt from the Regulations.

The Regulations have limited impact in respect of equal access to occupational pension because an employer may be able to justify the different treatment on objective grounds provide it is unrelated to sex.

There is no need for the employee to establish any less favourable treatment based on sex discrimination unlike claims under the Equal Pay Act 1970.

The Regulations do not apply to external recruitment but if an employee is denied a job on the basis that they want to work part time or job-share, this may constitute indirect sex discrimination.

For more information and compliance guidance on the Regulations, see www.dti.gov.uk/er/ptqa.htm.

Telecommunications (Lawful Business Practice) (Interception of Communications) Regulations 2000

The above Regulations were enacted pursuant to the Regulation of Investigatory Powers Act 2000. The Regulations came into force on 2 October 2000. The purpose of the Regulations is to make it lawful for businesses to intercept communications without consent from the employee.

An employer may lawfully monitor or record communications (reg. 3(1)) on their telecommunications systems without the consent of the employee if it needs to establish certain facts:

- related to the business (e.g. the agreed terms of a contract);
- for regulatory reasons (whether internal or external);
- for quality control or staff training;
- to prevent or detect a crime or fraud;
- to investigate unlawful use of the system (e.g. abuse of e-mails); or
- to monitor effective running of the system (e.g. to check for computer viruses).

Further, an employer may monitor (but not record) without consent communications relevant to the business (e.g. when an employee is off sick) or telephone calls made to an anonymous and confidential support helpline (e.g. to protect or offer support to welfare helpline workers).

△ Employers should take all reasonable efforts to warn staff that their communications may be monitored (reg. 3(2) Lawful Business Practice Regulations 2000). Communications that are clearly private (unless there has been an abuse of usage) and non-business related should not be intercepted as to do so may be a breach of a right to a private and family life (Sched. 1 art. 8 Human Rights Act 1998).

At the time of writing, there is a draft Code of Practice on the use of personal information in employer/employee relationships issued by the Information Commissioner. This is due to be finalised in late 2001.

Fixed Term Employees (Prevention of Less Favourable Treatment) Regulations 2001 (draft)

The above Regulations are still only in draft form and have been implemented pursuant to the EC Directive on Fixed Term Work (99/70/EC). The UK had to implement the Directive by 10 July 2001 with a 12 month extension if 'special difficulties arise'. The consultation process ended on 31 May 2001.

The Regulations will seek to ensure that fixed term employees are not treated less favourably than a comparable non-fixed term employee engaged in the same or broadly similar work in respect of terms and conditions of employment or be subject to a detriment. The employee must find a comparator who is a permanent employee based at the same establishment, if not, at a different workplace.

The employer may be able to rely on a defence of justification in respect of any different treatment.

The Regulations also provide that where an employee has been employed for four years or more either in a single contract or a series of contracts without a break, the employee will be treated as a permanent employee. Continuity of employment will be preserved by the employee in this event but the significance of this is minor given that the qualifying period for unfair dismissal has been reduced from two years to one year. Further, the Regulations state that an employer must have 'objective justification' when renewing a fixed term contract.

The Regulations also place an obligation on an employer to notify a fixed term employee of any suitable vacancies arising which are not of a fixed term nature. An employee whose rights have been infringed may ask the employer for written reasons for the less favourable treatment and may have grounds to institute an unfair dismissal claim.

⌂   It is useful to note that the draft Regulations will apply only to employees, not workers (but this position may change after the consultation period).

The Regulations do not apply to any differentials in pay and pensions but the anomaly is that it applies to contractual benefits such as contractual holiday pay and sick pay.

Employers should audit the existing workforce to ensure that employees working under fixed term contracts are not on less favourable terms to those enjoyed by permanent staff. Although pay and occupational pension schemes are excluded from the Regulations, contractual benefits given to permanent employees (e.g. health care and company car) have to be reassessed in the light of the Regulations. Any differentials and reasons for the employer's action should be documented. If there are any internal vacancies for permanent positions, the employer should notify all fixed term employees by way of circulars or the intranet.

For further information, see www.dti.gov.uk/er/fixed

CHAPTER 5

Employee's claim

5.1   GENERAL PRINCIPLES IN CONTRACT

The most common remedy for breach of contract is damages. Given that an employment contract is a contract to provide personal services, the courts are reluctant to compel the parties to continue with the contract if the parties no longer wish to do so. For this reason, the equitable remedies of specific performance and injunction are rarely exercised where damages would be adequate. Where the employer is a public body and the employee is a holder of public office, judicial review of the employer's decision on the basis that it is *ultra vires* may be sought as a public law remedy.

The purpose of damages in contract is to put the parties in a position they would have been had the contract been performed (i.e. to fulfil the expectation interest of the parties provided that the loss is not too remote).

The issue here is twofold: what is the type of loss that is recoverable by the aggrieved party and to what extent is the employer liable for those losses.

For the loss to be recoverable, it must have 'fairly and reasonably been considered arising naturally from the breach within the contemplation of both parties' (*Hadley* v. *Baxendale* (1854) 9 Ex. 341). To put it in another way, the loss is said to have arisen naturally if there was a 'serious possibility, real danger or very substantial probability' that it would occur (*Koufos* v. *Czarnikow* (*C*) (*The Heron II*) [1969] 1 AC 350). If the aggrieved party has any special losses, the other party is only liable if they were aware of the special circumstances of the aggrieved party (*Victoria Laundry* (*Windsor*) v. *Newman Industries Coulson & Co.* (Third Parties) [1949] 2 KB 528, CA).

☞ Employees should ask themselves:-

- is the loss claimed reasonably foreseeable between the parties at the time of contract? If not, it is too remote and not recoverable;
- has the employee mitigated his losses?

In respect of the type of loss recoverable for wrongful dismissal, the position has been laid down by the House of Lords in the case of *Addis* v. *Gramophone Co Ltd* [1909] AC 488. Here the employee was wrongfully dismissed and claimed for damages under the following heads:

(a) loss of salary for the notice period;

(b) reasonable commission for the notice period;

(c) damages for loss of reputation;

(d) damages for the humiliating manner of dismissal.

A majority of the House of Lords held that only categories (i) and (ii) were recoverable losses. Since then, the position in respect of losses sustained in category (iii) has changed (see 5.8) although category (iv) remains a loss that is unrecoverable in wrongful dismissal claims.

Damage limitation

In the employment contract context, and for the purposes of wrongful dismissals however, the employer's liability for the damages would be limited to a 'damages period'. This may comprise:

- contractual notice period;
- balance of a fixed term contract if there is no break clause for premature termination;
- statutory notice period;
- reasonable period in the event that a statutory period does not apply.

The courts assume that the employer is entitled to bring to an end the contract 'in the way that is most beneficial to himself, that is to say, that he would have determined the contract at the earliest date at which he could properly do so' (*Gunton* v. *Richmond upon Thames London Borough Council* [1980] 3 All ER 577) or in the manner least

77

onerous to the employer. This means that the employee's loss ends when the employer could have terminated the contract lawfully (*Alexander* v. *Standard Telephone & Cables Ltd* (*No. 2*) [1991] IRLR 280). In this respect, the law is concerned with legal obligation rather than expectations. An employee who has been given notice of termination is 'unlikely to be a source of future generosity to the employer (the "Lavarack principle")' (*Lavarack* v. *Woods of Colchester* [1967] 1 QB 278).The 'Lavarack principle' may well hold water if the employee has been dismissed without notice so that the employer is presumed to wish to dismiss the employee in any event. But where the employer has committed a repudiatory breach of contract, it does not necessarily follow that termination with notice is the next step an employer would take or that such a step is necessarily in the employer's best interest.

A different approach was taken by the High Court in Australia (*Commonwealth of Australia* v. *Amann Aviation Property Ltd* (1991) 174 CLR 64) where damages were awarded to an employee beyond the notice period and for losses representing lost chance of a renewal of the fixed term contract. The additional loss was based on general contractual principles and rules of remoteness, i.e. whether the loss was reasonably within the contemplation of the parties.

In English law, damages for wrongful dismissal are limited to the notice period. This contrasts with damages for unfair dismissal which may be awarded beyond the notice period and up to a period when the Tribunal takes the view that the employee should have found alternative employment subject to mitigation (the 'just and equitable' measure).

The fact that damages for wrongful dismissal seem to be confined to the notice period only should not be undermined as senior employees often have contractual notice periods for termination of up to two years. This may go some way in enabling the employee to recover further compensation which exceeds the statutory maximum of £51,700 where the employee's dismissal is both unfair and wrongful.

Mitigation

An employee cannot sit back and wait for their losses to accumulate but must take reasonable steps to seek alternative employment. Any earnings from their alternative employment and social security benefits will be taken into account when assessing the employee's damages for termination. Where the employee has found a permanent job that is equivalent (*Courtaulds Northern Spinning Ltd* v. *Moosa* [1984] IRLR 43) or better paid (*Fentiman* v. *Fluid Engineering Products Ltd* [1991] IRLR 150), this may result in a nil loss which has the effect of exonerating the former employer. In any event, the employee will be entitled to full loss of earnings from the date of termination until the start of the new job and need not retrospectively give credit from the new earnings in respect of the unemployment period. Where the employee has found alternative employment but is not as well paid as his previous job, his financial loss would be the difference between the two jobs.

The employee's obligation to mitigate their losses only applies to damages for breach of contract. These may include:

- compensation for failure to provide notice;

- compensation for failure to follow a contractual procedure;

- any discretionary payments upon termination, e.g. a golden handshake;

- compensation for loss of contractual benefits during the notice period, e.g. private use of company car, bonuses and profit related pay.

Where compensation clearly arises from the employee's contractual entitlement (e.g. an express right to a payment in lieu of notice, accrued wages or accrued holidays – regarded as a contractual debt) these are emoluments (rather than damages) and so are not subject to mitigation. However, emoluments are subject to tax and NI contributions under s.19 (Sched. E) of the Income and Corporation Taxes Act 1988.

Confusion may sometimes arise over whether a payment is in fact damages or emoluments. Getting it wrong may impact on any tax liability on sums paid out by an employer or received by an employee (see 5.11).

Let us now look at the possible heads of claim.

5.2   LOSS OF EARNINGS

Damages for loss of earnings are normally restricted to 'contractual notice pay'. This includes salary, commissions, bonuses and gratuities payable during the notice period. Where there is a fixed term contract, damages may be limited to the balance of the unexpired term if there is no break clause. In the case of *Clark* v. *BET plc* [1997] IRLR 348, the employee was able to claim anticipated salary increases as part of his damages for loss of earnings.

Although damages are generally restricted to the notice period, this may be considerable where the employee is a senior executive under a service agreement with notice provisions of up to 24 months. A percentage deduction may be made by the court or tribunal to account for the employee's accelerated receipt.

5.3 CONTRACTUAL, STATUTORY OR REASONABLE NOTICE PAY

Where the employer has failed to give the relevant notice for termination to the employee, it would be liable for damages to the employee subject to the employee's mitigation.

Employment contracts often contain a clause which allows the employer to effect a payment in lieu of notice (PILON). Where the contract expressly provides that the employment may be terminated by the employer on payment of a sum in lieu of notice, such a summary dismissal is a lawful act and not a breach of contract.

There are four types of PILON payments (*Delaney* v. *RJ Staples* (t/a De Montfort Recruitment) [1992] ICR 483):

(1) Express clause providing payment in lieu of notice (deemed as wages (*EMI Group Electronics Ltd* v. *Coldicott* (*Inspector of Taxes*) [1999] IRLR 630, CA)).

(2) Discretionary clause or discretionary payment in lieu of notice (deemed as damages).

(3) No express clause but the employer agrees to pay the employee in lieu of notice upon termination and the employee agrees to accept that payment (deemed as damages).

(4) No express clause but the employer pays the employee for the notice period without the employee's consent (deemed as damages).

If there is a payment in lieu of notice clause, check whether the clause is discretionary or absolute. If it is discretionary, the employee does not have an absolute or contractual entitlement in which case any payment would be deemed as damages and subject to mitigation. Therefore, if the employee has found alternative employment, any subsequent earnings must be accounted for to the former employer so that the actual loss of the employee is established (*Cerberus Software Ltd* v. *Rowley* [2000] IRLR 160, CA).

If the PILON is a contractual entitlement in the form of an agreed damages clause, then it is deemed as a contractual debt and should be paid net of tax and NI deductions as an 'emolument' (*Abrahams* v. *Performing Rights Society Ltd* [1995] IRLR 487).

In drafting a PILON clause, the employer should decide whether it wishes to confer an absolute right or a discretionary right of payment to the employee. An absolute right to effect payment in lieu allows the employer to summarily end the contract (without liability for wrongful dismissal) without prejudicing the enforceability of any restrictive covenants (*Rex Steward Jefferies Parker Ginsberg Ltd* v. *Parker* [1988] IRLR 483).

A discretionary right on the other hand means that the employer will have to allow the employee to work out the notice period unless a PILON is made. However, where the employee is on a high salary with a long notice period and has been wrongfully dismissed, this may benefit the employer in that any damages payable for the notice period would be subject to the employee's mitigation (i.e. the employee may be expected to secure alternative employment quickly).

The employer should decide whether the PILON clause is to be confined to notice pay or whether it also includes all benefits the employee is entitled under the notice period. If benefits are excluded, the employee may sue for them as damages

The facts of a recent Court of Appeal case are worthy of mention here (*Cerberus Software Ltd* v. *Rowley* [2001] IRLR 160). Mr Rowley was a sales and marketing director for the employer. Relations with the managing director broke down four years after he started work and the employer was intent to get rid of Mr Rowley on grounds of misconduct. Mr Rowley was summarily dismissed but this was later found by a Tribunal to be unlawful as the allegations were unjustified. Mr Rowley's contract provided that he was entitled to six months notice for termination and that the employer *may make a payment in lieu of notice*. However, Mr Rowley had found alternative employment which paid him £215 more per month than what he was originally getting.

The issue was whether he had an absolute entitlement to a PILON or whether it was discretionary.

A majority of the court held that the use of the word 'may' did not confer an absolute entitlement. If it was an absolute contractual entitlement, it would be regarded as a contractual debt and thus payable in net as wages. As it was only a discretionary payment, the claim was for damages for breach of contract (for failing to provide Mr Rowley with his six months notice). Damages for wrongful dismissal are subject to mitigation and the employee is required to minimise his loss. As Mr Rowley had earnings from his new employment, this had to be accounted for. The court therefore held that the original award by the Employment Appeal Tribunal for £21,348.21 (notice pay in gross) be set aside and for an appropriate amount to be substituted.

Where there is no contractual notice period, the maximum statutory entitlement is 12 weeks for those employees with 12 or more years of service (see 4.16). Such payment would be deemed as damages for termination and therefore paid in gross and subject to mitigation.

🖑 Employees should note that any payments from the employer in respect of sick pay, statutory sick pay, maternity pay, statutory maternity pay, holiday pay, sickness and injury benefit may be used to set off any statutory liability in respect of the minimum statutory notice pay (ss.88–91 ERA 1996).

Where there is no contractual notice so that a statutory notice period may apply, the employee may argue that they are entitled to reasonable notice and damages should be calculated in accordance with what is a reasonable period for the employee concerned (see 4.16).

5.4   FAILURE TO FOLLOW CONTRACTUAL PROCEDURES

If there is a contractual disciplinary and grievance procedure and the employer has failed to abide by it, the employee who has been dismissed for misconduct or incapability may claim damages for:

(a) how long it would have taken the employee to go through that procedure (*Gunton* v. *Richmond-upon-Thames LBC* [1980] IRLR 321, CA); and

(b) the lost chance of continued employment had the procedure been followed (*Raspin* v. *United News Shops Ltd* [1999] IRLR 9, EAT).

In respect of damages for failure to follow a contractual disciplinary procedure, damages would be assessed on the length of time the employer would have taken to complete the procedure and then damages are added for the notice period when the employer may lawfully terminate the contract.

Damages for 'lost chance' of continued employment is more difficult to prove or assess as the employer is presumed to be entitled to terminate the contract by notice in any event. Further, the employer may seek to argue that following the contractual procedure would have made no difference to the decision to dismiss (*Polkey* v. *AE Dayton Services Ltd* [1987] IRLR 503). If this is the case, there may be no award for lost chance of continued employment.

⌂ Employers should ensure that their disciplinary and grievance policy is not contractual but for guidance only to avoid a wrongful dismissal! However, for the purposes of avoiding an unfair dismissal claim, employers should still have regard for the ACAS Code on Disciplinary and Grievance Procedures before dismissing employees for misconduct or incapability.

5.5 LOSS OF USE OF COMPANY CAR, MOBILE PHONE, INTEREST FREE LOANS AND OTHER COMPANY PERKS

An employee may be able to claim for the loss of private use of a company car if this was allowed in the contract of employment (*Shove* v. *Downs Surgical plc* [1984] 1 All ER 7). No claim may be made if the car was strictly for business use only. In determining what is the employee's loss, the Tribunal may take into account the following:

- weekly share of the road tax, insurance premium and cost of petrol between the parties;
- cost of hiring a replacement car for private use;
- average mileage cost by reference to the make, age and engine size of the vehicle as published by AA or the RAC. This may range between £50 and £100 per week.
- Inland Revenue scale rates for car and fuel.

If the employee is not required to contribute towards the costs of running the car, the employee's claim for loss will be more substantial.

For a breakdown on what is the average cost per mile of running a vehicle, go to the AA website: www.theaa.co.uk/motoringandtravel/motorcosts/. The cost per mile will depend on the engine size and type of fuel used.

The Inland Revenue scale rates are designed for tax purposes in respect of the value of car perks but are preferred by employers in view of its more conservative valuations. Note however that this method of calculation is not always accepted by the Tribunals because it may not adequately reflect the employee's loss.

Table 4 Inland Revenue Car Fuel Scale Charges 2001–2002

Engine cylinder	Petrol	Diesel
1400 cc or less	£1,930	£2,460
1401 cc to 2000 cc	£2,460	£2,460
More than 2000 cc	£3,620	£3,620
Unclassified capacity	£3,620	£3,620

In respect of loss of use of mobile phone, employees should work out what is the value of the private usage over the damages period.

In respect of interest free loans, employees should calculate what is the 'interest free' element of the benefit that they would have had over the damages period.

Other benefits such as subsidised mortgage, private health insurance, gym membership, free meals and free or subsidised accommodation should be assessed with reference to their value or costs of making equivalent arrangements for the damages period. Employees should be ready to convert company perks into monetary terms when quantifying losses under this head.

5.6   LOSS OF PENSION RIGHTS

It was recently held by the Court of Appeal in *Silvey* v *Pendragon plc* [2001] EWCA Civ 784, CA that where an employee was dismissed twelve days before he reached his fifty-fifth birthday and had lost accrued pension rights, this was a recoverable loss In that case, the employee was wrongfully dismissed in that he was summarily dismissed for redundancy (i.e. without notice) and given pay in lieu of notice when the contract did not allow the employer to do so (see 2.2 on effective date of termination and PILON).

Where pension loss is a recoverable head of damage, the loss would be confined to the value of the employee's pension at the date of dismissal and what it would have been at the expiry of the notice period.

Where the loss relates to a final salary scheme (defined benefits scheme), the Tribunal will measure the difference between the value of the deferred pension (i.e. capitalised value) at the date of dismissal and that at the end of the damages period. With a final salary scheme, the value of the pension is based on a percentage of the employee's final salary *at retirement* regardless of the level of contributions made. The percentage applied is dependent on the employee's years of service and the scheme accrual rate (generally 1/60 or 1/80 of final salary for each year of service). So if an employee earns a salary of £50,000 and has worked for five years and the accrual rate is 1/80, the pension at the date of unlawful termination would be 5/80 × £50,000 or £3,125. If the employee is entitled to one year of notice for termination, then the pension entitlement at the date of lawful termination would be 6/80 × £50,000 or £3,750. The loss for the damages period is therefore £625.

In the case of a money purchase scheme (defined contributions scheme), the loss will depend on the total contributions of the employee including the contributions they would have got during the notice period. The employee's loss may be calculated in the following ways:

- the basis of lost employer's contributions for the notice period (if the scheme is capable of being transferred to a new employer);
- a return of all contributions made up to the expiry of the damages period;
- a comparison is made between the value of the investment by the relevant fund managers as at the time of the termination and the end of the damages period.

In all cases, an allowance has to be given for mitigation, possibility of withdrawal from the scheme (e.g. if the employee could have left the employer during the damages period), absence of the employee's contribution during the notice period and accelerated payment.

○ Employees are advised to seek specialist advice as this area is highly complex. The Industrial Tribunal Compensation for loss of pension rights booklet published in 1991 by the HMSO may be of some assistance but the EAT has called for new guidelines for assessing pension loss (*Clancy* v. *Cannock Chase Technical College and another* [2001] IRLR 331, EAT).

5.7 LOSS OF RIGHT UNDER PROFIT SHARING SCHEMES, PROFIT RELATED SCHEMES AND SHARE OPTION SCHEMES

In a profit sharing scheme, shares are purchased by trustees with contributions from the employer and held by trustees on behalf of employees. The loss would be assessed with reference to the value of the shares at the expiry of the damages period.

A profit related pay scheme is dependent on the profitability of the employer's business and an employee may claim damages for what is due to him during the damages period.

In respect of share option schemes, reference must be made to the rules of the scheme (*Levett* v. *Biotrace International plc* [1999] IRLR 375). Is there an exclusion clause for compensation for lost rights (*Micklefield* v. *SAC Technology Limited* [1991] 1 All ER 275)? It is common for share option schemes to provide that the right to exercise any option lapses upon termination of employment. Such an exclusion will not be caught by the Unfair Contract Terms Act 1997 if the company is registered in England and Wales, as a share option scheme is a contract for the creation of securities and therefore exempt from the Act. The exclusion of an employee's right to compensation for loss of the right to exercise their share option upon termination is void if the share option relates to a company registered in Scotland (s.23 Unfair Contract Terms Act 1977 (which only applies in Scotland)).

If the employee has a contractual entitlement to a share option, then damages may be assessed on the basis of the market value of the shares if the option had been exercised at the expiry of the damages period.

Where the employee is entitled to a discretionary share option scheme during employment or after termination, the employee may claim for loss of a chance to exercise the share option. However, where it can be shown that the lost chance has no value in that the employer would not have exercised the discretion in view of the employee's conduct, no damages may be awarded (*O'Laoire* v. *Jackel International Ltd (No. 2)* [1991] ICR 718).

5.8 MENTAL ANGUISH, STIGMA DAMAGES AND LOSS OF CAREER PROSPECTS

The law of contract does not generally award damages for distress unless the purpose of the contract is to provide pleasure, relaxation and peace of mind (*Bliss* v. *South East Thames Regional Health Authority* [1985] IRLR 308). Therefore there is no award for psychological damage arising from the manner in which an employee has been dismissed (*Addis* v. *Gramophone Co Ltd* (1909) AG 488). However, it has been held (*Malik* v. *BCCI SA* (In liquidation) [1998] AC 20) that where the employer is involved in fraudulent activities during the employment relationship such that its employees are implicated or disadvantaged following termination of employment, the employer may be liable for 'stigma damages'. Mere dishonesty on the part of the employer is not an automatic breach of trust and confidence. The court will look at the degree of the employer's dishonesty and the number of employees affected to ascertain whether the reputation of the employees could have been tainted by the employer's conduct. The employee must prove actual (not hypothetical) financial loss to claim 'stigma damages'.

A distinction is drawn so that stigma damages by way of pecuniary losses caused by the employer's breach of contract (e.g. breach of trust and confidence) when the employee is still employed, is recoverable, whereas damages for hurt feelings as a result of wrongful dismissal, i.e. the manner of dismissal, are not. The implied term of trust and confidence is concerned with the preservation of the continuing employment relationship and not for use in connection with the termination of employment.

In a recent House of Lord's decision, the majority of the court accepted that social conditions have changed so that it is inappropriate to equate a contract of employment with commercial contracts. However, policy arguments rule against the award of damages for the manner of dismissal at common law as the reasonableness of a dismissal and any losses flowing from that are already enshrined in unfair dismissal legislation (*Johnson* v. *Unisys Ltd* [2001] IRLR 279, HL). Currently, the compensatory award for unfair dismissal is based on what is 'just and equitable' by reference to the fairness or unfairness of the employer's dismissal. This may arguably also take into account any humiliation, distress or damage to reputation caused by the manner of dismissal.

Employers who participate in wrongful or fraudulent trading should note that they risk a potential claim by senior executives for 'stigma damages'.

☞ Stigma damages may be available for wrongful dismissal claims if such a loss is caused by the employer's breach of trust and confidence during the employment relationship. Stigma damages may also be awarded in unfair dismissal claims as part of the compensatory award taking into account the manner of dismissal.

⌂ In discrimination cases, the employee may be able to claim aggravated damages (the motive and manner in which the employer has carried out the unlawful act) and compensation for injury to feelings. This may range from a low award of £500 (*Alexander* v. *The Home Office* [1988] IRLR 190, CA) to a medium award of £20,000 (*HM Prison Service* v. *Salmon* [2001] IRLR 425, to a high award of £45,000 (*Yeboah* v. *Crofton & Hackney LBC* [1999] 86 EOR 21).

Where the purpose of the contract is not solely to provide a wage or salary but to train a person (e.g. an apprentice (*Dunk* v. *George Waller & Son Ltd* [1970] 2 QB 163)) or to preserve or promote one's reputation (e.g. actors (*Marbé* v. *Edwardes* (*George*) *(Daly's Theatres)* [1928] 1 KB 269, CA)), the aggrieved party may seek damages for damage to career prospects.

5.9   LOSS OF OPPORTUNITY TO CLAIM UNFAIR DISMISSAL/REDUNDANCY

An employee who does not have the necessary one year of service to bring an unfair dismissal claim may be able to do so via the back door. In misconduct or incapability dismissals, if it can be shown that had the employer followed its own contractual disciplinary procedure so that the employee would have had the necessary service, the Tribunal may award the lost chance of an unfair dismissal claim, subject to a deduction of the claim not succeeding.

Thus, where an employee has been dismissed with notice which expired three weeks short of one year of service necessary to claim unfair dismissal, and the dismissal is wrongful in that the employer has failed to abide by its contractual disciplinary procedure, the exhaustion of which would have enabled the employee to achieve one year of service, damages may be awarded for the loss of opportunity to sue for unfair dismissal (*Raspin* v. *United News Shop Ltd* [1999] IRLR 9). Damages would be assessed based on whether the employee could have remained employed, been fairly dismissed or been unfairly dismissed. A percentage reduction in the damages is made based on the speculation.

Note however that where there is no wrongful dismissal in that there is an express clause authorising the employer to terminate with pay in lieu of notice, the employee is relieved of working out the notice period so that no time is 'clocked up'. This head of damage is thus limited where the employer is not in breach of contract (*Morran* v. *Glasgow Council of Tenants Associations* [1998] IRLR 67)

    Employers should ensure that their disciplinary and grievance procedure is NOT contractual so that an employee who falls short of one year of continuous service does not use the procedure to accumulate the necessary qualifying period to sue for unfair dismissal.

    Employers may also consider using fixed term contracts of less than 12 months at the first instance so that an employee has no right to claim unfair dismissal (*Booth* v. *United States of America* [1999] IRLR 16). The draft Fixed Term Employees (Prevention of Less Favourable Treatment) Regulations 2001 are only designed to prevent less favourable treatment in respect of employment terms and conditions, not statutory rights.

    Where the employee can show that there is a real risk that he would be made redundant during the notice period, he may be entitled to redundancy payment in whole or in part (*Basnett* v. *Jackson (J&A) Ltd* [1976] ICR 63, QB.

5.10 OVERLAP WITH DAMAGES FOR UNFAIR DISMISSAL

The law only seeks to compensate the employee for their actual losses. If an employee has two claims against the employer, i.e. wrongful and unfair dismissal, the employee will not be able to claim twice for their losses. For example, if the employee has claimed notice pay under the wrongful dismissal head, this will be deducted from the compensatory award in the unfair dismissal claim. See Appendix 5 for a Schedule of Loss.

5.11 DAMAGES, TAX AND SOCIAL SECURITY CONSIDERATIONS

Should an employee be compensated in gross or net?

The general rule is that an employee should be put in the position had the employer not breached the contract. Thus, the employee should not be in a position where they are in fact in a better financial position as a result of the employer's breach. For this reason, damages awarded by the Courts and Tribunals are net of income tax and NI contributions (*British Transport Commission* v. *Gourley* [1955] 2 All ER 796). This is known as the 'Gourley principle'. There is however nothing to stop the employer from offering the employee gross compensation either for good industrial reasons or as an incentive to the employee not to pursue legal proceedings.

Payments made on termination of an employee's service fall into one of the categories for tax purposes:

- payments are taxable in full (emoluments);
- payments which are taxable but only if they exceed £30,000 (s.188 Income and Corporation Tax Act 1988) (damages);
- payments which are completely tax free (they are not emoluments and are under £30,000).

Emoluments and tax

Emoluments of office or employment are taxable under s.19 Sched. E of the Income and Corporation Taxes Act 1988. These 's.19 termination payments' include:

- wages or salary;
- sick pay, maternity pay, income support;

- non cash vouchers and credit tokens;
- the value of the benefit of low rent or rent-free accommodation;
- the value of sport and recreational facilities;
- a gain on the exercise of a share option (approved schemes involving shares with a value of £30,000 or less are exempt);
- pensions;
- a 'golden hello' at the start of employment referable to future services;
- a sum paid in return for the employee entering into a restrictive covenant not to compete with the employer upon termination of the contract (s.313 Income and Corporation Taxes Act 1988);
- a 'golden handshake' at the termination of employment paid under the terms of a contract.

Income Tax

Tax is payable as follows for the tax year ending 5 April 2002:

£0–£1,880	10% (lower rate)
£1,881–£29,400	22% (basic rate)
over £29,400	40% (higher rate)

There are allowances given to the employee before tax is applied.

	£
Personal allowance	4,535
Personal allowance (age 65–74)	5,990
Personal allowance (75 and over)	260
Married couples allowance (65–74)	5,365
Married couples allowance (75 and over)	5,435
Blind persons' allowance	1,450
Married allowance	2,070
Children's tax credit	5,200

There is a residual right to married couples allowance provided the employee is born before 6 April 1935 In othci cases, married couples allowance hao been abolished.

National Insurance Contributions

Employees earning less than £72 per week (Lower Earnings Limit) are exempt from NI payments.

Employees earning between the Lower Earnings Limit and £87 per week (Employee's Earning Threshold) are exempt from NI payments but are still entitled to claim benefits as if they have paid Class 1 contributions.

Employees earning £87 per week and more (Employee's Earnings Threshold) are subject to NI deductions. The employee pays NI at the rate of 10 per cent of £87.01 to £575 (Upper Earnings Limit) if the employer has not contracted out of the State Earnings Related Pension Scheme (SERPS) and the employer pays 11.9 per cent on earnings above £87 per week. For employees who contract out of the state pension scheme and subscribe to a final salary scheme or a money purchase scheme, the employer's rate of NI payment is discounted by 3 per cent and 0.6 per cent respectively.

Employees and Directors with emoluments of £8,500 or more a year are also taxed on any loan advanced by the employer (interest saved by comparison with an official rate), private use of company car, cost of child care facilities provided by the employer and private use of business mobile phone.

If an employee earns £40,000 per annum, deduct their tax allowance accordingly. With the taxable balance, the first £1,880 will be taxed at 10 per cent, from £1,881 to £29,400 is taxed at 22 per cent and the remainder is taxed at 40 per cent.

Damages and tax

Damages for termination of contract which are not 'emoluments of employment or office' (i.e. a contractual entitlement) are not subject to tax under Sched. E or National Insurance deductions in the usual way. These 's.148 termination payments' may include:

- genuine redundancy payment (statutory (s.579 ICTA 1988) or contractual);
- compensation for unfair dismissal;
- damages for wrongful dismissal (notice pay, failure to follow contractual procedure, ex-gratia payments, loss of contractual benefits);
- a discretionary/gratuitous payment on termination (golden handshake).

These payments are tax free if they do not exceed £30,000 (s.188 Income and Corporation Taxes Act 1988). Any lump sum termination payment that is in excess of £30,000 is subject to tax but only in respect of the excess (s.148 Income and Corporation Taxes Act 1988).

If the employee has received compensation net of tax but the total settlement still exceeds £30,000, the employee may be subject to tax again. To avoid the employee being taxed twice, the employer should compute what is the excess taxable for the damages period and 'top up' the net settlement. This will neutralise the situation.

△ If the employer has an express liquidated damages clause which provides that in the event of unlawful termination, the employee will receive a payment, this may be treated by the parties as damages and therefore a s.148 termination payment free of tax. The Inland Revenue may, however, treat such a payment as a s.19 termination payment and subject to tax and NI since it is paid pursuant to an express clause. NI ceases to be payable when employment ceases but if a payment is treated as a s.19 termination payment, then NI will be deductible nonetheless. Employers should always obtain a tax indemnity from the employee in the event of uncertainty.

Mixture of emoluments and damages

Compensation for termination often comprises different elements. The compensation may include payments pursuant to the terms and conditions of employment and damages for termination of contract. The employer would be well advised to isolate the components accordingly for tax purposes in the event of having to account to the Inland Revenue. Any sums paid to the employee which arise as a contractual entitlement must be paid net of tax as wages. Any other non-contractual payment may be paid in gross as damages for termination. Even so, employers should be mindful of the £30,000 tax free ceiling.

Where a Tribunal or court declares that an employee has been wrongfully dismissed and makes an order for damages, the employer should again separate the components that make up the compensation accordingly as tax and NI may have to be deducted where applicable.

△ For further information, see www.inlandrevenue.gov.uk/pdfs/ emp2000/cw92_2000.pdf

If an employer wishes to pay the employee gross, it should ensure that it has an indemnity from the employee in the event that the employer is being pursued by the Inland Revenue if tax is payable on any of the components (see Appendix 6).

Damages and social security

Damages recovered from unfair and wrongful dismissal must take into account any jobseeker's allowance obtained by the employee while unemployed since termination of employment up to the date of the tribunal's decision including damages awarded to represent the employee's future loss (Employment Protection (Recoupment of Jobseeker's Allowance and Income Support) Regulations 1996).

The receipt of a statutory redundancy payment or voluntary severance payment does not disqualify the employee from claiming jobseeker's allowance as the payment relates to past service (reg. 71 Jobseeker's Allowance Regulations 1996).

An employee who receives compensation from termination of employment (with the exception of accrued wages, holiday pay, maternity or sick pay, employment expenses, occupation pension and statutory redundancy) may be barred from claiming jobseeker's allowance for the period to which the compensation payment relates. The exclusion period will depend on whether payment was made in lieu of notice, for the balance of a fixed term contract, the period for statutory consultation on collective redundancies or may be measured by dividing the terminal payment by a 'week's pay' for statutory purposes (reg. 94(6) Jobseeker's Allowance Regulations 1996).

CHAPTER 6

Employer's counterclaim

6.1 FAILURE TO PERFORM CONTRACTUAL DUTIES

Where the employee has not performed any of his contractual duties, they are not entitled to their contractual wages. An employer is therefore allowed to make a lawful deduction of wages when an employee goes on strike (s.15 Employment Rights Act 1996; *Miles* v. *Wakefield Metropolitan District Council* [1987] ICR 368). Where the employee has failed to perform his full contractual duties, the employee is again not entitled to his full contractual salary (*Wiluszynski* v. *Tower Hamlets LBC* [1989] IRLR 259). An employer is entitled to withhold or deduct a sum from the employee's wages representing his financial loss as a result of the employee's breach. Unless the contract provides otherwise, a day's wage is calculated by reference to a calendar day (1/365) rather then a working day (1/240) of the employee's annual salary (s.7 Apportionment Act 1870, *Taylor* v. *East Midlands Offender Employment* [2000] IRLR 760).

6.2 REIMBURSEMENT OF FEES FOR TRAINING COURSES/PROFESSIONAL QUALIFICATIONS

It is common for employers to stipulate that it may sponsor an employee on a training course or the pursuit of a professional qualification related to the job for which employee has been employed. However, where there is an express provision that the employer should be reimbursed, in part or full, for fees incurred on behalf of the employee if the employee should leave the employer within a period of time after completing the course, this should be clawed back from the employee.

It has, however, been held by the Court of Appeal that an express clause requiring the employee to pay significant sums of money to the employer, upon the employee's termination of the contract within specified periods of completing a training programme, may be unenforceable as being in restraint of trade (*Electronic Data Systems* v. *Hubble* (1987), IDS Brief 363.

⚠ To avoid an express clause from being unenforceable, employers should ensure that any reimbursement sought is reasonable and adequately reflect the employer's loss. Any refunds should be expressed as proportions diminishing the longer the employee has worked for the employer after the end of the sponsored training.

6.3 NOTICE PERIOD

An employee who has resigned without giving the employer the relevant notice period or refused to work out the notice period may put the employer in a difficult spot. Obtaining an injunction may be possible but is often not the appropriate solution. Some employers have therefore resorted to the use of liquidated damage clauses requiring the employee to compensate the employer a sum representative of the notice period. Such a clause must be an adequate reflection of the employer's loss and not act as a penalty to the employee (*Giraud UK Ltd* v. *Smith* [2000] IRLR 763) penalty clauses being unenforceable at common law (*Dunlop Pneumatic Tyre Co* v. *New Garage and Motor Co.* [1915] AC 79).

⚠ Ensure that the liquidated damages clause is a genuine pre-estimate of the employer's loss. The sum needs to reflect adequately damages payable by the employee for the wrongful termination. Has the employer suffered a loss as a result of the employee's actions in the first place? It may be an idea to state that the employee will be liable for the cost of the employer in hiring someone for the notice period (subject to any savings the employer may make) and ensure that such deduction is in full and final settlement of all claims for the employee's breach.

6.4 EXCESS HOLIDAYS

If there is a contractual provision for deductions to be made in respect of excess holidays taken, this may be used as a set off against the employee's claim. Alternatively, the employer may be entitled to make deductions if there has been an overpayment of holiday pay such a deduction will not constitute an unlawful deduction of wages (s.13 ERA 1996).

6.5   EXCESS EXPENDITURE

If the employee has claimed excess expenditure over that they are entitled to, the employer may claw it back as an overpayment (s.14 Employment Rights Act 1996) and this will not constitute an unlawful deduction of money even though there is no express clause in the contract which allows the employer to do so (*Discount Tobacco and Confectionery Ltd* v. *Williamson* [1993] ICR 37).

6.6   BREACH OF RESTRICTIVE COVENANTS

An employee may be in breach of covenants during employment or after termination of the contract. Where the breach is committed while the employee is still employed (a repudiatory breach), it could be argued that the employer is discharged from performing his obligations under the contract if he accepts the employee's breach. If the employee has breached the contract, then they are not entitled to enforce any of the contractual terms (e.g. notice or notice pay). If the employee's conduct is serious, it may qualify as gross misconduct justifying summary dismissal.

⚠   A liquidated damages clause may cover a situation such as this so that the employer is compensated for any loss resulting from the employee's breach. See 6.8 on 'moonlighting'.

If an employee is in breach of restrictive covenants, the employer make ask the court to award damages but the loss is not easily quantifiable in some cases or may not be an adequate remedy. Employers then have the option of asking the court for interim relief by way of an injunction to restrain the employee's breach. Whether an interlocutory injunction (a temporary injunction until the matter is resolved at the main trial) will be granted by the court will depend on whether the balance of convenience lies in favour of an injunction or not (*American Cyanamid Co* v. *Ethicon* [1975] AC 396). The employer would also be required to give the court a cross undertaking to make good any loss caused to the employee if it subsequently proves that the injunction should not have been granted. The court will examine the financial standing of the employer before granting an injunction.

An injunction is an equitable remedy (a discretionary remedy) so that if an employer withholds material from the court which is relevant to the case, an injunction may not be granted. There is a maxim that those who come before equity must come with clean hands!

Where the employee is in possession of property or confidential information belonging to the employer material, the employer may apply for a search order and require the employee to deliver up the items in question. A search order is only granted in exceptional circumstances.

⚠ Where an employer has committed a repudiatory breach of contract, e.g. where it has made an unlawful deduction of wages or where there has been a breach of trust and confidence prior to the termination of contract, the restrictive covenants become unenforceable (*General Billposting Co* v. *Atkinson* [1909] AC 118). An employer who is in breach of contract cannot enforce the contract against the employee. The employer cannot therefore apply for an injunction in the High Court to restrain the employee although the employee is in breach of the restrictive covenants.

However, it has been held that where the employee has received monies in lieu of notice, then the employee does not have any outstanding claim against the employer. The employer's breach is not deemed 'repudiatory' so the covenants remain enforceable (*Konski* v. *Peet* [1915] 1 Ch 530).

⚠ Employees who have resigned and launched a constructive dismissal claim against the employer may affect the employer's enforceability of any restrictive covenants.

6.7 COMPANY EQUIPMENT

Employees are increasingly given fringe benefits such as the use of a company car, mobile phone and lap-top. If the employee has damaged, lost or failed to return company property, the employer should counterclaim for the value of the equipment or cost of repair. Reserve an express clause in the contract to deal with this eventuality and quantify your loss.

6.8 BREACH OF IMPLIED TERM OF FIDELITY AND AN ACCOUNT FOR PROFITS

An employee is allowed to do what they wish in their spare time but this is subject to three exceptions:

(a) the employee must not enter into competition with the employer's business (*Hivac Ltd* v. *Park Royal Scientific Instruments Ltd* [1946] Ch 169);

(b) the employee's external engagements must not affect the employee's discharges of his usual duties to his employer;

(c) if the employee also owes a fiduciary duty to the employer (e.g. if the employee is also a director and therefore owes a duty to the shareholders (*Industrial Development Consultants* v. *Cooley* [1972] WLR 443) or where the employee holds confidential information) he is required to account for any secret profits.

Therefore, an employee who competes with their employer in their spare time would be in breach of the implied term of fidelity. Remedy for such a breach would be damages if loss could be proved.

Where there is an express clause requiring an employee to maintain confidentiality and the employee is in breach of confidence, is there a remedy if the employer is unable to substantiate his loss for breach of contract? The issue here is whether it is then possible for the employer to ask the employee to account for his secret profits (i.e. to disgorge the entire profits).

An account for profits is not an ordinary remedy for breach of contract but a remedy in restitution. Where a person is in a fiduciary relationship or in breach of confidence, he is required to restore any property or money received to the rightful owner where their receipt is unjustified. An account of profits therefore ensures that the person is not unjustly enriched or has retained an unjust advantage.

It has recently been held that where the employee has breached their contractual obligations not to divulge official information after the employment ceased, he may be held accountable to his employer for profits made from his autobiography containing what was once confidential information (*Attorney General* v. *Blake and another* [2001] IRLR 36) . The House of Lords cautioned that such a restitutionary remedy is not readily available in a breach of contract claim unless the employer had a legitimate interest in preventing the employee's profit making activity and hence depriving him of his profit or if the employee is found to be in flagrant breach of his contractual obligations. If the information divulged is confidential, the employee will owe the employer a fiduciary duty and an account for profits will be a remedy as a matter of course.

It was recently held that where a director resigned taking with him employees of the previous employer and diverted part of the latter's business opportunities to his new company, the director in doing so is in breach of his fiduciary duty so that he is principally liable to account for profits. Equally, the directors of the new company who exploited business opportunities of the previous employer are liable to account (*CMS Dolphin Ltd* v. *Simonet and another* (2001) Employment Lawyer Issue 67, HC)

⌂ Ensure that there is an express clause requiring the employee to account for profits made in breach of contract even if the employer is unable to quantify its loss for damages.

Where there is no competitive activity, there is no duty of fidelity unless the employee is also a director and therefore owes a fiduciary duty.

However, it has been held that where a senior employee has profited from the work carried out by the junior employees of the employer, the employer may claim that a fiduciary duty arises from the employment relationship so that the profiteering employee is made to account for profits (*University of Nottingham* v. *Fishel* [2000] IRLR 471). An employee may therefore owe a fiduciary duty where specific contractual obligations place the employee in a position where they must act solely in the best interest of the employer.

CHAPTER 7

Effecting termination/dismissal

7.1 EMPLOYEE'S RESIGNATION

Where the employee is of the view that the employer has failed to perform its common law or statutory duties (s.13(5) Employment Relations Act 1999), they may invoke the grievance procedure at the workplace in an attempt to try and resolve matters. The employer may be in breach of its obligations if, for example, there has been an unlawful variation of contractual terms, bullying in the workplace or failure to make reasonable adjustments if the employee is disabled. The ACAS Code of Conduct on Disciplinary and Grievance Procedure (Employment Code of Practice (Disciplinary and Grievance Procedures) Order 2000) provides that an employee/worker has a statutory right to be accompanied by a fellow worker/union official to a grievance hearing (s. 13 ERA 1999).

Where the employment relationship is beyond repair, the employee may be left with little option but to resign and take legal action against the employer. A resignation must be unambiguous so that words said in the heat of the moment while under emotional stress may not amount to a resignation.

If the contract provides that the employee is required to give notice of termination, failure to do so may render the employee liable to a claim for breach of contract.

However, it may not be necessary for the employee to provide the relevant notice for termination if it can be shown that the employer has committed a fundamental breach of contract so that the employee is entitled to resign and claim constructive dismissal.

A constructive dismissal may be with or without notice. Where the employee is seeking to argue that trust and confidence has completely broken down, it may be more appropriate to resign without notice to support the gravity of the employee's allegations (see 2.23). However, this invariably creates a problem for the employee if they have not secured alternative employment or are unlikely to do so in the foreseeable future.

Where the employee resigns for a reason unconnected to the employer's conduct, they are not dismissed and have no right to claim unfair or wrongful dismissal.

7.2   EMPLOYER'S TERMINATION/DISMISSAL

Breaking the news to the employee is not an easy or pleasant task. Careful planning is required in respect of which is the most appropriate strategy and this would depend on the circumstances and/or reason for the termination. It is important to ensure that someone of sufficient seniority is entrusted to deliver the news. The person effecting the termination/dismissal should be prepared to set out the background/events leading up to the employer's decision and to discuss any proposals for settlement, where applicable.

An employee with one year of service is entitled to written reason for dismissal within 14 days if one is requested (s.92(1) ERA 1996). The employer should ensure that the written reason given mirrors what is stated in the employer's Notice of Appearance as the employee may use the written reason for dismissal as evidence against the employer at the Tribunal.

Dismissal interview

The dismissal interview may be formal or informal. This would largely be dependent on the circumstances and/or reason for the termination/dismissal.

Summary dismissal

Where the employee is guilty of gross misconduct (e.g. theft, physical violence, bullying, property damage, serious insubordination, serious negligence, infringement of health and safety rules, serious breach of confidence), this may justify summary dismissal provided that the employer has carried out a reasonable investigation into the alleged misconduct.

Summary dismissal merely deprives the employee of the right to notice for termination; the employer is still required to honour obligations in respect of accrued rights up to the time of termination (e.g. accrued wages and untaken holidays).

Where the reason for termination is attributable to incapability of the employee despite prior warnings and offers for assistance, the employer may be justified in dismissing the employee.

Whether the dismissal is for misconduct or incapability, the ACAS Code on Disciplinary and Grievance Procedure provides that an employee has a right to be accompanied to a disciplinary hearing. A disciplinary hearing is a hearing held in connection with the employee's conduct or performance which results in the employer taking some form of action, including dismissal. The employer may wish to resolve matters on an informal basis (with no resultant sanction) in which case the right of accompaniment will not arise.

Where the employee has committed a gross misconduct justifying summary dismissal, it may be necessary to arrange for the employee to be escorted out of the employer's premises. Steps should be taken to facilitate this process in a manner which is least disruptive to the business, particularly if the employee is required to vacate their desk immediately in the presence of other employees.

Informal meeting

The employer should seek to ensure that termination does not expose them to any liability for wrongful or unfair dismissal. If there are grounds which may give rise to a potential claim, then it is vital to ensure that a commercial settlement is attractive enough for the employee to accept in full and final settlement of any breach of contract or of any other potential claim; so that there is no possibility of or incentive for the employee to seek redress through legal proceedings (see Chapter 8 on negotiating settlements).

In some cases, it may be more appropriate to give the employee notice for termination (and send the employee on garden leave where applicable) and then sort out a severance package during the notice period.

In other cases, the employer may wish to negotiate a settlement before giving the employee notice. The employee may be told informally of the company's decision to terminate and of proposed terms of settlement. 'Without prejudice' negotiations of this nature may open channels for negotiation between the parties without the termination or dismissal being acrimonious. The employer should seek to ensure that a severance package does what it says, i.e. it makes a clean break between the parties.

If the employee is also a director, note that the employee's directorship cannot be removed by the shareholders except by ordinary resolution on special notice (s.303 Companies Act 1985). Any compensation for loss of office to the director must be approved by shareholders (s.312 Companies Act 1985).

Formal termination

Where the reason for the termination/dismissal is due to the employee's incapability by reason of persistent poor performance, the employee may exercise their right to be accompanied to the disciplinary hearing. This may prejudice confidentiality and may further provoke embarrassment for the employee. It would therefore be prudent to warn the employee in advance of the nature of the meeting and inform them of their rights and to ascertain whether the employee would still wish to be accompanied.

Where the employer has committed a breach and decides to terminate the employee's employment in writing, it may wish to make a formal offer in full and final settlement of the employee's complaint with a view to avoiding court action. An 'on the record' offer for compensation may be made to the employee based on what they are legally entitled to by reference to the nature of the breach or termination. Unlike 'without prejudice' offers, 'on the record' offers may be referred to in evidence in legal proceedings and may be used by one party to show the unreasonable conduct of the other party. Any offer of settlement should be made without admission of liability.

   The employer is required to issue a P45 to the employee on termination of employment (reg. 23 Income Tax (Employments) Regulations 1993). The employer must also notify the Inland Revenue of any severance package which exceeds £30,000. Whereas the employee is only required to pay primary National Insurance contributions at 10 per cent of any excess above the

Employee's Earnings Threshold (£87 weekly) subject to the Upper Earnings Limit (£575 weekly), the employer's secondary contributions towards the NI Fund is based on 12 per cent of any sum above the Employee's Earnings Threshold without any ceiling applied.

7.3   SETTING THE RECORD STRAIGHT!

Following the employee's departure, it may be necessary to make a press statement to maintain staff morale, client confidence and public confidence in the employer's business. Where applicable, an internal statement (agreed between the employer and outgoing employee) should be circulated to members of the relevant department to preserve morale. Any statements made, whether internally or externally must not be defamatory.

Where the employee's termination/dismissal is also accompanied by their resignation of directorship, the employer, if it is a listed company, may be required to notify the relevant authorities such as the London Stock Exchange.

CHAPTER 8

Negotiating settlements in and out of court/Tribunal

8.1 RISK ASSESSMENT FOR THE EMPLOYER

- Establish the strengths and weaknesses of your own case.

- What are the strengths and weaknesses of the employee's case?

- Monitor the employment position of the employee, i.e. has the employee mitigated their loss by way of alternative employment? Check with employment agencies on the availability of work in the particular field which the employee was employed. The onus is on the employer to show that the employee has failed to mitigate their loss.

- If the employee is also claiming unfair dismissal, has there been unreasonable or contributory conduct by the employee so that any award ought to be reduced?

- Consider what are the upper and lower limits of the boundaries for settlement.

- Is a 'nuisance payment' suitable in the circumstances?

- Would settling the claim affect morale in the workplace and undermine the authority of the person who took the decision to terminate the employee's contract?

- Would settling the employee's claim set a precedent for future claims?

- Would adverse publicity from the proceedings affect recruitment of employees. Employers are generally concerned about bad publicity and employees may use this as leverage. However, employers should not readily submit to blackmail particularly when the threat relates to information unconnected to the proceedings.

- What is the cost to the employer of preparing for the hearing and mobilising witnesses?

- Bear in mind the litigation risk involved in any proceedings. The outcome of a case may depend on how your witnesses perform and the experience of the Tribunal or judge assigned to your case.

- Even if you have a strong case, some allowance must be made for the risk associated with litigation. Sometimes it may be more commercially expedient to settle than litigate.

8.2 RISK ASSESSMENT FOR THE EMPLOYEE

- Establish the strengths and weaknesses of your own case.

- What are the strengths and weaknesses of the employer's case?

- Is the reason for the employee's termination/dismissal an automatically unfair reason so that the employee has a claim for unfair dismissal without the necessary qualifying service?

- Does the employee want a monetary award or reinstatement/re-engagement?

- Does the employee have reliable witnesses who are prepared to testify on their behalf (see 4.23 on the Public Interest Disclosure Act 1998 which may help)?

- Will publicity of proceedings affect the employee's future employability?

- Will proceedings against the existing employer affect the quality of references sought by prospective employers (see 4.22)?

- If the employee is in gainful employment, what is the cost to the employee for taking time off work to attend the hearing?

- An award for dismissal from a tribunal is subject to recoupment (this does not apply to discrimination awards) (s.16 Employment Tribunals Act 1996). Where an employee has received any benefits in the form of Income Support or Jobseeker's Allowance from the state after the termination, it has to reimburse the state in the event of recovering any damages against the employer (Employment Protection (Recoupment of Jobseeker's Allowance and Income Support) Regulations 1996 (SI 1996 No. 2349)). The employer must therefore withhold the relevant sum from the employee in the award for compensation and pay it directly to the Department of Social Security. The effect of recoupment is to prevent an employee from recovering their losses twice.

☞ A wrongful dismissal claim is concerned with whether the employer is in breach of contract. It is not a vindication exercise. Even with unfair dismissal claims, the role of the Tribunal is not to prove the guilt or innocence of the employee but whether the employer has acted fairly in the dismissal.

8.3 COSTS

Costs are rarely awarded to a winning party or against a losing party in the Tribunal. This is often an incentive on employers to settle out of court as costs are unrecoverable in any event. New rules are now in place so that vexatious litigants may be ask to pay the employer's cost if a claim is unmeritorious or frivolous. A Tribunal has power to award up to £10,000 in this instance (Sched. 1 r. 14(3) The Employment Tribunals (Constitution and Rules of Procedure) Regulations 2001) (previously £500 (r. 12 Employment Tribunals (Constitution and Rules of Procedure) Regulations 1993)). Costs may be awarded in full or part, agreed between the parties or taxed by the county court or High Court in the absence of agreement (Sched. 1 r. 14(6) The Employment Tribunals (Constitution and Rules of Procedure) Regulations 2001).

In respect of actions in the county court or the High Court, costs follows the event and the loser pays the winner's costs. An employee will therefore think twice about proceeding to trial in the event of losing and having to pay the employer's costs. This risk should be used to the best advantage by the employer.

8.4 TACTICS FOR EMPLOYERS AND EMPLOYEES

Smokescreens

Capitalise on the strengths of your case and exploit the weaknesses of your opponent's case. Is it possible to cast a smokescreen?

Recoupment

Employers should maximise the effect of the recoupment regulations by doing a deal with the employee. If the employee has received benefits to the value of £1,000, an out of court settlement of £500 which will go directly into the pocket of the employee (and unrecouped) may save the employer £500 thereby benefiting both parties.

Discretionary payments

If the employer has a discretion to effect payment in lieu of notice, it may use this as a bargaining chip in negotiations with the employee. An offer to pay an employee for a specified period rather than for the employee to work out the notice is not an unattractive measure. Does the employer have a discretion to allow the employee to exercise share option rights upon termination of the employment? Is it possible to make an ex-gratia payment to the employee to ensure that a smooth departure is achieved? Employees should also capitalise on any discretionary benefits in the negotiation process.

Sweeteners

If the employee has privileges such as private use of a company vehicle, computer equipment, private health insurance and use of club facilities, is it possible to let the employee have continued usage for x number of months after termination? What about contributions towards the employee's legal costs?

Gross payments

An employee who is dismissed or whose contract is terminated is only entitled to compensation net of tax and NI contributions otherwise they would be unjustly enriched by the employer's breach ('the Gourley principle'). However, there is nothing to stop the employer from 'creaming the cake' by offering the employee *gross* compensation if the sum is up to £30,000. Anything in excess of £30,000 has to be paid in gross in any event as tax is payable (s.188 Income and Corporation Taxes Act 1988).

Part 36 offers

Where an employee's claim for wrongful dismissal is in excess of £25,000 and therefore has to be issued in the county court or High Court, a settlement may be reached by way of a Part 36 offer pursuant to the Civil Procedural Rules (Part 36 Civil Procedural Rules 1998). An employer may pay a sum of money into court to settle an employee's claim, so may an employee in settlement of the employer's counterclaim. Such offers may be made before or after proceedings have been issued. A Part 36 offer made by a defendant in the proceedings must be paid into court for it to be valid. It must be kept open for 21 days after which acceptance is only possible with the agreement of the parties or with the consent of the court. A Part 36 offer, if pitched properly, is a powerful catalyst towards settlement. This is because an offeree who eventually fails to beat the offeror's payment into court at trial is liable for the costs of the offeror from the latest date when the offer could be accepted. Employers and employees should consider the use of this weapon after proceedings have been issued.

△ A Part 36 offer only compromises the employee's common law claim for breach of contract. A compromise of the employee's statutory rights can only be achieved by way of a compromise agreement (see 8.5).

References

Since an employee does not have a legal right to a reference (save for certain circumstances), the employer may consider offering a reference to the employee as part of the settlement. Most employees are reliant on a reference to move on with their careers and this tactic should not be underestimated. Remember to stick to a factual reference to avoid potential liability as set out in 4.22.

By the same token, employees should ensure that a reference is part of any proposed settlement. Note however that some requests for references may be elaborate and may require the employer to go into details about the employee's conduct and reasons for departure from the employer.

ACAS

The involvement of ACAS as an independent and neutral conciliator after Tribunal proceedings have been instituted may prove useful in some instances. Where the employee is unrepresented, the use of ACAS to broker a settlement cannot be undervalued. The intervention of ACAS may open up channels for negotiation and a deal may be struck over the telephone much more swiftly than correspondence between the employer and employee which may delay matters unnecessarily. The service is also free.

☞ As of 21 May 2001, a new arbitration scheme has been introduced by ACAS for unfair dismissal claims. The scheme is voluntary and only applies where there is no dispute on jurisdiction and dismissal is accepted by the parties. The hearing is held in private and ACAS will pay the reasonable costs of hiring the room. Any award made by the arbitrator is enforceable in the civil courts. For more details, see www.hmso.gov.uk/si/si2001/20011185.htm or www.acas.org.uk.

If a settlement is reached with the help of ACAS, a COT3 agreement has to be entered between the parties. This is wider than a compromise agreement as the terms of settlement are in full and final settlement of *any* action, known or unknown, the employee may have against their employer in connection with their employment or termination thereof.

🖉 USEFUL PRECEDENT

The Employee agrees to accept the sum of [_____] in full and final settlement of all possible claims the employee may have against the employer, existing under statute, common law or in equity of whatsoever nature, whether known or unknown to the parties, within or outside the contemplation of the parties at the time of signature, including all rights which do not exist or could not currently be foreseen as existing, in connection with the employee's employment or termination thereof.

The House of Lords recently warned that if the employer wants to exclude all possible claims and to achieve 'so extravagant a result, they should . . . [use] . . . language that left no room for doubt and . . . [alert the employee] to the true effect'. (*Bank of Credit and Commerce International SA* v. *Ali* (No. 1) [2001] 2 WLR 735) Note however that it is not possible to exclude a claim for personal injury resulting from the employer's negligence (see also s.2(1) UCTA 1977).

The scope of claims capable of being compromised by ACAS are set out s.18 Employment Tribunals Act 1996 (as amended). These include s.2(1) of the Equal Pay Act 1970, s.63 of the Sex Discrimination Act 1975, s.54 of the Race Relations Act 1976, s.8 of the Disability Discrimination Act 1995, ss.64, 68, 137, 138, 146, 168, 169, 170, 174, 188, 190 of the Trade Union and Labour Relations (Consolidation)

Act 1992, Parts V, VI, VII and X of the Employment Rights Act 1996 and proceedings in respect of which a tribunal has jurisdiction (s.18(1)(e) Employment Tribunals Act 1996). As of 1 May 2001, rights under the Part-Time Workers (Prevention of Less Favourable Treatment) Regulations 2000 may be excluded (Part Time Workers (Prevention of Less Favourable Treatment) Regulations 2001).

An agreement reached orally with ACAS is binding even though it is not in writing (s.203(2)(e) ERA 1996). However, employers should ensure that the employee's representative has been authorised to enter into the COT3 agreement for and on behalf of the employee, otherwise the settlement is void (*Gloystarne & Co Ltd* v. *Martin* [2001] IRLR 15, EAT). Those advising employers should check that the employee's representative is named on the ET3 form, and that the ET3 form has been signed by the employee. If not, ensure that the representative obtains a written authority from the employee before concluding matters. A legal representative who acts without the authority of the employee may be liable to the employer for breach of warranty of authority.

8.5 SETTLEMENTS OUT OF COURT/TRIBUNAL

Wrongful dismissal claims may be settled out of court without any formality. So long as the agreement is supported by consideration, the contract is enforceable in so far as it relates to the employee giving up their common law rights.

However, where the employee is agreeing to give up their statutory rights to bring a claim in a Tribunal (e.g. unfair dismissal), this must comply with certain statutory requirements. An agreement by an employee to 'contract out' of their statutory rights must take the form of a COT3 Agreement (see 8.4) or a compromise agreement (s.203(2)(e)(f) Employment Rights Act 1996).

For a compromise agreement of statutory claims (without the intervention of ACAS) to be valid (s.203(3) ERA 1996), it must:

(a) be in writing;

(b) relate to the particular complaint (i.e. the subject of the dispute);

(c) the employee must have received independent legal advice from a qualified lawyer as to the effect of the employee's ability to pursue their rights before an Employment Tribunal. The restriction to 'qualified lawyers' has been changed since August 1998 so that officers, official employees and members of an independent trade union and voluntary workers at advice centres may advise the employee (Sched. 1 Employment Rights (Dispute Resolution) Act 1998 incorporating s. 203(3A) ERA 1996) provided that:

- the adviser is covered by a professional indemnity insurance in respect of any advice given;
- the adviser is identified;

(d) the compromise agreement must confirm that the above conditions are satisfied.

It is not possible to compromise all of the employee's statutory rights. The rights that are capable of being contracted out are set out in s.77(4) of the Sex Discrimination Act 1975, s.72 of the Race Relations Act 1976, s.9(2) of the Disability Discrimination Act 1995, s.230(3)(1)(f) of the Employment Rights Act 1996, s.288(2A) of the Trade Union and Labour Relations (Consolidation) Act 1992, s.49(3) of the National Minimum Wage Act 1998, reg. 35(2)(b) of the Working Time Regulations 1998, and reg. 8 of the Part-Time Workers (Prevention of Less Favourable Treatment) Regulations 2001.

Employers should ensure that the terms of settlement contain a confidentiality clause which prevents the employee from discussing the terms with any third party, whether the public or other fellow employees. Note, however, that where the dispute relates to discrimination, the Commission for Racial Equality (which acts for the employee) is unable to enter into a 'no publicity' clause as they have a statutory obligation to inform the public.

   ⚠   Ensure that any compromise agreement has the appropriate 'gagging clause' (see Appendix 6).

Ensure that the scope of the claims the employee is compromising is clear (*Dattani v. Trio Supermarkets Ltd* [1998] ICR 872, CA). A compromise in respect of the employee's contractual rights is not governed by any legal rules so long as it is supported by consideration. However, a compromise of the employee's statutory rights (e.g. redundancy payment, unfair dismissal, discrimination, equal pay, rights pursuant to a transfer of undertakings) must comply with the legal requirements set out above otherwise it is void (*Sutherland v. Network Appliance Ltd and another* [2001] IRLR 12) (see Appendix 5).

Note, however, that a compromise agreement is only a compromise of any further action the employee may have against the employee in respect of a particular complaint. An employee cannot compromise their rights in respect of any potential claim which is not the subject of the complaint or is unknown to the employee at the particular time.

A compromise agreement is thus narrower than a COT3 Agreement which provides a blanket protection to the employer in respect of 'all possible claims' the employee may have against the employer in connection with his employment or termination thereof. However, a COT3 Agreement may only be used if ACAS is involved in the resolution of the dispute.

It is not uncommon for employees to ask the employer to contribute towards their legal costs in seeking advice from an independent adviser usually between £300–£500. A qualified lawyer is either a barrister or a solicitor. Note, however, that where the advice is given by an advice centre worker, this must be free but a union may apparently charge for its services.

Where the parties have entered into a compromise agreement in respect of a wrongful termination claim and the terms of the agreement have not been performed, the Employment Tribunal has jurisdiction to enforce it (*Rock-It Cargo Ltd* v. *Green* [1997] IRLR 581, EAT).

APPENDICES

Ready reckoner for calculating the number of week's pay due

Read off the employee's age and number of complete years' service. The table will then show how many weeks' pay the employee is entitled to. (The table starts at 20 because no one below this age can qualify for a redundancy payment.) The table can also be used to calculate the basic award for unfair dismissal.

If the employee is aged between 64 and 65, the amount due should be reduced by one twelfth for every complete month that the employee is over 64.

Age (years)	Service (years)																		
	2	3	4	5	6	7	8	9	10	11	12	13	14	15	16	17	18	19	20
20	1	1	1	1	—														
21	1	1½	1½	1½	1½	—													
22	1	1½	2	2	2	2	—												
23	1½	2	2½	3	3	3	3	—											
24	2	2½	3	3½	4	4	4	4	—										
25	2	3	3½	4	4½	5	5	5	5	—									
26	2	3	4	4½	5	5½	6	6	6	6	—								
27	2	3	4	5	5½	6	6½	7	7	7	7	—							
28	2	3	4	5	6	6½	7	7½	8	8	8	8	—						
29	2	3	4	5	6	7	7½	8	8½	9	9	9	9	—					
30	2	3	4	5	6	7	8	8½	9	9½	10	10	10	10	—				
31	2	3	4	5	6	7	8	9	9½	10	10½	11	11	11	11	—			
32	2	3	4	5	6	7	8	9	10	10½	11	11½	12	12	12	12	—		
33	2	3	4	5	6	7	8	9	10	11	11½	12	12½	13	13	13	13	—	
34	2	3	4	5	6	7	8	9	10	11	12	12½	13	13½	14	14	14	14	—
35	2	3	4	5	6	7	8	9	10	11	12	13	13½	14	14½	15	15	15	15
36	2	3	4	5	6	7	8	9	10	11	12	13	14	14½	15	15½	16	16	16
37	2	3	4	5	6	7	8	9	10	11	12	13	14	15	15½	16	16½	17	17
38	2	3	4	5	6	7	8	9	10	11	12	13	14	15	16	16½	17	17½	18
39	2	3	4	5	6	7	8	9	10	11	12	13	14	15	16	17	17½	18	18½
40	2	3	4	5	6	7	8	9	10	11	12	13	14	15	16	17	18	18½	19
41	2	3	4	5	6	7	8	9	10	11	12	13	14	15	16	17	18	19	19½

	Service (years)																		
Age (years)	2	3	4	5	6	7	8	9	10	11	12	13	14	15	16	17	18	19	20
42	2½	3½	4½	5½	6½	7½	8½	9½	10½	11½	12½	13½	14½	15½	16½	17½	18½	19½	20½
43	3	4	5	6	7	8	9	10	11	12	13	14	15	16	17	18	19	20	21
44	3	4½	5½	6½	7½	8½	9½	10½	11½	12½	13½	14½	15½	16½	17½	18½	19½	20½	21½
45	3	4½	6	7	8	9	10	11	12	13	14	15	16	17	18	19	20	21	22
46	3	4½	6	7½	8½	9½	10½	11½	12½	13½	14½	15½	16½	17½	18½	19½	20½	21½	22½
47	3	4½	6	7½	9	10	11	12	13	14	15	16	17	18	19	20	21	22	23
48	3	4½	6	7½	9	10½	11½	12½	13½	14½	15½	16½	17½	18½	19½	20½	21½	22½	23½
49	3	4½	6	7½	9	10½	12	13	14	15	16	17	18	19	20	21	22	23	24
50	3	4½	6	7½	9	10½	12	13½	14½	15½	16½	17½	18½	19½	20½	21½	22½	23½	24½
51	3	4½	6	7½	9	10½	12	13½	15	16	17	18	19	20	21	22	23	24	25
52	3	4½	6	7½	9	10½	12	13½	15	16½	17½	18½	19½	20½	21½	22½	23½	24½	25½
53	3	4½	6	7½	9	10½	12	13½	15	16½	18	19	20	21	22	23	24	25	26
54	3	4½	6	7½	9	10½	12	13½	15	16½	18	19½	20½	21½	22½	23½	24½	25½	26½
55	3	4½	6	7½	9	10½	12	13½	15	16½	18	19½	21	22	23	24	25	26	27
56	3	4½	6	7½	9	10½	12	13½	15	16½	18	19½	21	22½	23½	24½	25½	26½	27½
57	3	4½	6	7½	9	10½	12	13½	15	16½	18	19½	21	22½	24	25	26	27	28
58	3	4½	6	7½	9	10½	12	13½	15	16½	18	19½	21	22½	24	25½	26½	27½	28½
59	3	4½	6	7½	9	10½	12	13½	15	16½	18	19½	21	22½	24	25½	27	28	29
60	3	4½	6	7½	9	10½	12	13½	15	16½	18	19½	21	22½	24	25½	27	28½	29½
61	3	4½	6	7½	9	10½	12	13½	15	16½	18	19½	21	22½	24	25½	27	28½	30
62	3	4½	6	7½	9	10½	12	13½	15	16½	18	19½	21	22½	24	25½	27	28½	30
63	3	4½	6	7½	9	10½	12	13½	15	16½	18	19½	21	22½	24	25½	27	28½	30
64	3	4½	6	7½	9	10½	12	13½	15	16½	18	19½	21	22½	24	25½	27	28½	30

Offer letter

The offer letter should include the following conditions:

The Company offers you the position of [————————].

This offer is subject to the following: (*Delete where applicable)

REFERENCES

This offer is subject to the Company receiving satisfactory references from the referees you have nominated in your job application form. This conditional offer will be withdrawn in the event that references received by the Company are unsatisfactory or if references are not provided.

ABILITY TO START WORK WITHOUT RESTRICTIONS

This offer is conditional upon you being able to commence work on [————————] and you confirm that you are free from any restrictive covenants from your previous employer.

QUALIFICATIONS

This offer is subject to you possessing the relevant qualifications as set out in [*the job application form*] and you producing evidence of your qualifications.

DRIVING LICENCE

It is a condition of this job that you possess a valid driving licence without which you are prohibited from using any vehicle belonging to the Company.

MEDICAL EXAMINATION

This job offer is subject to you attending a medical examination to ensure that you are fit to carry out the duties assigned to you. A medical appointment has been arranged for you on [————————].

WORK PERMITS

It is illegal for the Company to employ a non-EU national without a valid work permit. This offer is conditional upon your work permit application by the Company being successful if one is necessary.

CONFIDENTIALITY

It is a condition of this job that you sign and return the Confidentiality Agreement contained in this letter by [————————].

PROBATIONARY PERIOD

The first [————] months of your employment is a probationary period. Your contract may be terminated during this period with [————] weeks' notice in the event that your performance or conduct is unsatisfactory. If the employment is considered satisfactory, this will be confirmed in writing at the end of your probationary period.

PLACE OF WORK

Your place of work is at [————————]. However, you accept that you may from time to time, be required to work at any other establishment of the Company subject to reasonable notice if need be.

SALARY AND BENEFITS

Your starting salary will be [————————].
If you remain employed by the Company after the probationary period, your salary will be [————————].
Further, you will be entitled to [————————————].

I accept that the offer of employment in this letter is subject to the conditions mentioned herein.

Signed: .... (Employee)

Date : ....

Written statement of employment particulars

The s.1 written statement is not in itself a contract of employment. However, it may be used to evidence, as with an offer letter, what were the agreed terms between the employer and employee.

1. You [*employee*] began employment with [*employer*] on [*date*].

2. Your previous employment with [*company*] which began on [*date*] does/does not count towards your continuity of employment for the purposes of statutory protection.

3. You are employed as a [*job title*] or a brief description of the work for which you have been employed is [*see attached job specification*].

4. Your place of work is [*address*] but you may be required to work at [*other addresses*] if need be. Your employer's address is [————————].

5. Your pay will be [—————] payable [*in arrears by* —————].

6. Your hours of work are [————————].

7. Your holiday entitlement is [————————].

8. In the event that you are sick and incapacitated for work, you will be entitled to [*contractual sick pay/statutory sick pay*].

9. Details of the Company's pension schemes are found in [—————].

10. During your probationary period, the Company may terminate your contract with [———] weeks' notice. You may terminate your contract with the Company with [———] weeks' notice during the probationary period. After the probationary period, the contract may be terminated by either party with [———] weeks' notice.

11. Your employment is [*permanent*] [*temporary and expires on x*] [*fixed term of x months expiring on* ————].

12. The collective agreements which directly affect your terms and conditions of your employment are [*identify the agreements*].

13. You will be/not be required to work outside the United Kingdom. If you are required to work abroad, you will be paid in [*currency*] and will be entitled to [*benefits*]. The terms relating to your return to the United Kingdom are [————].

14. The rules relating to the Company's Disciplinary and Grievance policy are [*explain*]. If you are unhappy with any disciplinary decision which affects you or if you have a grievance, you may raise your concern with [————].

15. A contracting out certificate under the Social Security Pension Act 1975 is/is not in force for the employment this statement is being made.

Quantifying damages for wrongful dismissal

Calculate what is the damages period
Contractual notice period?   **1**
Statutory notice period?
Reasonable period?
Balance of fixed term contract (if no break clause)?

DAMAGES FOR WRONGFUL TERMINATION
Multiply [1] by

Loss of pay by reference to damages period
Loss of overtime pay, bonuses, commission,
interest-free loans
Loss of private use of company car   **A**
Loss of pension rights (e.g. lost contributions
if a money purchase scheme)

_____

Loss of profit sharing scheme, profit related
scheme and share option scheme
Loss of pension rights (e.g. value of final salary
scheme at termination date and end of damages
period or in the case of a Money Purchase Scheme,
a return of all contributions paid to date or value
of investment fund at termination date and end of
damages period)
Loss of wages for time taken to follow contractual
procedure
Failure to give employee notice before termination
Loss of opportunity to claim unfair
dismissal/redundancy   **B**
Loss of career prospects/stigma damages

_____

LESS
Employee's mitigation of loss:

- earnings from new employment during notice period
- social security payments
- ex-gratia payments
- any compensatory award for unfair dismissal
  (if it also covers notice pay and benefits to avoid   C
  double recovery)   ————————

Employee's gross damages after mitigation   D

If D exceeds £30,000, the employee has to pay tax
on the excess at the higher rate of 40 per cent.

NET LOSS NOT SUBJECT TO MITIGATION
(EMOLUMENTS)
Back Pay (accrued wages)
Contractual Holiday Pay   E
Contractual Payment In Lieu of Notice   ————————

Employee total loss is D + E   F

LESS
Employer's counterclaim (where applicable):

- failure to carry out contractual duties – pay cut
- reimbursement of training courses
- liquidated damages clause
- excess holidays/expenditure
- company equipment
- account for accounts
- employer's counterclaim for damages for breach
  of restrictive covenants   G
                                                           ————————

Employer's pay out to employee   F – G

Quantifying damages for unfair dismissal

BASIC AWARD

Current maximum (20yrs × £240 per week × 1.5)
(s.277(1)(a) Employment Relations Act 1999)   **£7,200**

LESS
- unreasonable refusal of reinstatement/re-engagement
  (s.122(1) ERA 1996)
- conduct before dismissal (s.122(2) and (3) ERA 1996)
- redundancy payment/award (s.122(4) ERA 1996)   **A**

COMPENSATORY AWARD   **£51,700**

Current maximum £51,700 (s.124(1) Employment
Relations Act 1999 which promulgated the Employment
Rights (Increase of Limits) Order 2001 (SI 2001/21))

PRESCRIBED ELEMENT SUBJECT TO RECOUPMENT (LOSS OF EARNINGS UP TO DATE OF TRIBUNAL'S DECISION)

Net wages from date of dismissal to date of assessment
Stigma damages (possibly)

LESS

- payments in lieu of notice
- earnings in alternative employment

LESS

- mitigation
- 'polkey deductions' (%)
- contributory fault of employee (s.123(6) ERA 1996)
- conduct before dismissal (s.123(1) ERA 1996)   **B**

NON-PRESCRIBED ELEMENT

Future loss of earnings
Loss of other benefits (before and after hearing)
Loss of statutory rights
Loss of contractual redundancy payment in excess of
statutory redundancy payment (s.123(3) ERA 1996)
Loss of pensions
Stigma damages (possibly)
Expenses

LESS
Any other payments made by employer (e.g.wrongful
dismissal)
Excess of redundancy payment over basic award

LE/SS

- mitigation
- 'polkey deductions'
- contributory fault of employee (s.123(6) ERA 1996)   **C**

ADDITIONAL AWARD

Breach of reinstatement /re-engagement order
(s.277(1)(b) Employment Relations Act 1999)   **D**

(26 weeks to 52 weeks' pay – £6,240 to £12,480)   ————

Employer's pay out to employee   **A+B+C+D**

☞ Polkey deductions and contributory fault are not deducted from the
basic award. Such deductions are only made from the compensatory
award. Polkey deduction must be made first before deductions for
contributory fault (*Digital Equipment Co Ltd* v. *Clements (No. 2)*
[1998] IRLR 34). If a percentage deduction is applied in either
case, they should be made in respect of all elements of the compensatory award so that the level of recoupment is accurate.

127

APPENDIX 6

Compromise agreement

BETWEEN:

1. [*Employer*] whose registered office is at [——————] ('the Company');

AND

2. [*Employee*] of [——————] ('the Employee').

WHEREAS:

(A) The Company and the Employee have agreed to enter into this Agreement upon reaching terms with the Employee upon his departure from the Company.

(B) The Employee confirms and acknowledges that before entering into this Agreement he/she has received independent advice from a relevant independent advisor, namely [——————] as to the terms and effect of the Agreement, in particular as to the effect of the Agreement upon his ability to pursue any complaint before an Employment Tribunal.

IT IS AGREED THAT:

1. Within [——] days of

    (i) the Company's receipt of the Employee's signed acceptance of these terms, an acknowledgement as set out in Schedule 1 of the Agreement from the relevant independent advisor to the Employee,

(ii) the Company will pay to the Employee a payment of
[——————] comprising:
[——————]

2. The Employee will be responsible for all and any liability for tax and National Insurance contributions payable in respect of the monies received by the Employee under Clause 1.

3. In consideration of Clause 1 above, the Employee agrees that these terms are offered by the Company without any admission of liability and are in full and final settlement of all claims in all jurisdictions which the Employee may have against the Company or any associated company or any of their offices or employees however so arising and whether in connection with his employment with the Company or its termination on [date] including without limitation any claim for [a redundancy payment], [unfair dismissal], [claim under the Part-time Workers (Prevention of Less Favourable Treatment) Regulations 2001], [Human Rights Act 1998], [wrongful dismissal], [discrimination on any ground], [equal pay] and any other breach of any [contractual] or [statutory] right.

4. The Employee and the Company agree to maintain as secret and confidential the terms of this Agreement and the circumstances concerning the termination of the Employee employment, save where such disclosure is necessary or appropriate to the Employee's professional advisors, or the Inland Revenue.

5. The relevant independent advisor has confirmed to the Employee that he/she is a qualified person as defined in the Employment Rights (Dispute Resolution) Act 1998 and that he/she or his/her organisation has a policy of insurance in force covering the risk of a claim by the Employee in respect of any loss arising in consequence of his/her advice.

6. The Company and the Employee hereby agree to refrain from passing any adverse or derogatory comment upon each other or from taking part in any conduct conducive or potentially conducive to the bringing of the Company, its directors or employees, or the Employee into disrepute.

7. It is agreed that conditions regulating Compromise Agreements under Section 203 of the Employment Rights Act 1996, [Section 77

129

of the Sex Discrimination Act 1975], [*Section 72 of the Race Relations Act 1976*], [*Section 9 of the Disability Discrimination Act 1995*], [*Section 77 of the Equal Pay Act 1970*], [*Section 288 of the Trade Union and Labour Relations (Consolidation) Act 1992*], [*s.49 of the National Minimum Wage Act 1998*], [*Regulation 35(2) of the Working Time Regulations 1998*] and [*Regulation 8 of the Part-Time Workers (Prevention of Less Favourable Treatment) Regulations 2001*] have been satisfied.

8. The Employee's advisor will sign and deliver to the Company an Advisor's Certificate in the form attached as Schedule I to this Agreement.

9. This Agreement shall be governed by and construed in accordance with English law.

Signed [———————]   Dated [————]

For and on behalf of the Company

Signed [———————]   Dated [————]
The Employee

Signed [———————]   Dated [————]
The Employee's Advisor

SCHEDULE I

Acknowledgement

I acknowledge receipt of the Compromise Agreement of which the above is a copy and of the sum of [——————] referred to in it.

I confirm that I have taken independent advice from [——————————] and I confirm and agree to the terms set out in the Compromise Agreement.

Signed [————————————]   Date of Signature [——————————]

I [*Employee's Advisor*] of [—————————————] confirm that [*Employee*] has received independent legal advice within the meaning of Section 203(4) of the Employment Rights Act 1996 as to the terms and effect of the Compromise Agreement of which the above is a copy and in particular its effect on his ability to pursue his rights before an Employment Tribunal. I am a relevant independent advisor as defined in ERDRA 1998 Schedule 1 at the time I gave the advice referred to, and there is, and was at the time I gave the advice, in force a policy of insurance covering the risk of a claim by [*Employee*] in respect of any loss arising in consequence of the advice I gave.

Signed: [*Employee's Advisor*]

Directory

ACAS ENQUIRY HELPLINES
http://www.acas.org.uk/

Birmingham
Warwick House,
6 Highfield
Birmingham B15 3ED
0121 456 5856

Bristol
Regent House
27A Regent Street
Clifton
Bristol BS8 4HR
0117 946 9500

Cardiff
3 Pubeck House
Lambourne Crescent
Llanishen
Cardiff CF4 5PH
029 2076 1126

Fleet
Westminster House
Fleet Road
Fleet
Hampshire GU13 8PD
01252 811868

Glasgow
Franborough House
123–157 Bothwell Street
Glasgow G2 7JR
0141 204 2677

Leeds
Commerce House
St Alban's Place
Leeds LS2 8HH
0113 243 1371

Liverpool
Cressington House
249 St Mary's Road
Gaston
Liverpool L19 0NF
0151 427 8881

London
Clifton House
83–117 Euston Road
London NW1 2RB
020 7396 5100

Manchester
Boulton House
17–21 Chorlton Street
Manchester M1 3HY
0161 228 3222

Newcastle upon Tyne
Westgate House
Westgate Road
Newcastle upon Tyne NE1 1TJ
0191 261 2191

Nottingham
Anderson House
Clinton Avenue
Nottingham NG5 1AW
0115 969 3355

EMPLOYMENT TRIBUNALS IN ENGLAND, WALES AND SCOTLAND

Employment Tribunal Service
Enquiry Line: 0845 795 9775

Aberdeen
Inverlair House
West North Street
Aberdeen AB9 1AL
Tel: 01224 643307
Fax: 01224 631551

Ashford
Tufton House
Tufton Street
Ashford TN23 1RJ
Tel: 01233 621346
Fax: 01233 624423

Bedford
8–10 Howard Street
Bedford MK40 3HS
Tel: 01234 351306
Fax: 01234 352315

Birmingham
Phoenix House
1–3 Newhall Street
Birmingham B3 3NH
Tel: 0121 236 6051
Fax: 0121 236 6029

Bury St Edmunds
100 Southgate Street
Bury St Edmunds IP33 2AQ
Tel: 01284 762171
Fax: 01284 706064

Bristol
The Crescent Centre
Temple Back
Bristol BS1 6EZ
Tel: 0117 929 8261
Fax: 0117 925 3452

Cardiff
2nd Floor, Caradog House
1–6 St Andrews Place
Cardiff CF1 3BE
Tel: 029 2067 8100
Fax: 029 2022 5906

Dundee
13 Albert Square
Dundee DD1 1DD
Tel: 01382 221578
Fax: 01382 227136

Edinburgh
54–56 Melville Street
Edinburgh EH3 7HF
Tel: 0131 226 5584
Fax: 0131 220 6847

Exeter
Renslade House
Banhay Road
Exeter EX4 3BX
Tel: 01392 279665
Fax: 01392 430063

Glasgow
Eagle Building
215 Bothwell Street
Glasgow G2 7TS
Tel: 0141 204 0730
Fax: 0141 204 0732

Leeds
4th Floor, Albion Tower
Albion Street
Leeds LS1 5ES
Tel: 0113 245 9741
Fax: 0113 242 8843

Leicester
5A New Walk
Leicester LE1 6TE
Tel: 0116 255 0099
Fax: 0116 255 6099

Liverpool
Union Court
Cook Street
Liverpool L2 4UJ
Tel: 0151 236 9397
Fax: 0151 231 1484

London Central
19–29 Woburn Place
London WC1H 0LU
Tel: 020 7273 8575
Fax: 020 7273 8686

London South
Montague Court
101 London Road
West Croydon CR0 2RF
Tel: 020 8667 9131
Fax: 020 8649 9470

Manchester
Alexandra House
14–22 The Parsonage
Manchester M3 2JA
Tel: 0161 833 0581
Fax: 0161 832 0249

Newcastle upon Tyne
Quayside House
110 Quayside
Newcastle upon Tyne NE1 3DX
Tel: 0191 232 8865
Fax: 0191 222 1680

Nottingham
3rd Floor, Byron House
2A Maid Marion Way
Nottingham NG1 6HS
Tel: 0115 947 5703
Fax: 0115 950 7612

Reading
5th Floor, 30–31 Friar Street
Reading RG1 1DY
Tel: 0118 959 4917
Fax: 0118 956 8066

Sheffield
14 East Parade
Sheffield S1 2ET
Tel. 0114 276 0348
Fax: 0114 276 2551

Shrewsbury
Prospect House
Belle Vue Road
Shrewbury SY3 7NR
Tel: 01743 358341
Fax: 01743 244186

Southampton
3rd Floor, Duke's Keep
Marsh Lane
Southampton SO14 3EX
Tel: 023 8071 6400
Fax: 023 8063 5506

Stratford
44 The Broadway
Stratford E15 1XH
Tel: 020 8221 0921
Fax: 020 8221 0398

Watford
3rd Floor, Radius House
51 Clarendon Road
Watford
Hertfordshire WD1 1HU
Tel: 01923 281752
Fax: 01923 281781

EMPLOYMENT APPEALS TRIBUNAL

Audit House
58 Victoria Embankment
London EC4Y 0DS
Tel: 020 7273 1041
Fax: 020 7273 1045
Internet:
http://www.employmentappeals.gov.uk/

COMMISSION FOR RACIAL EQUALITY (CRE)

Elliot House
10–12 Allington Street
London SW1E 5EH
Tel: 0207 828 7022
Internet: http://www.cre.gov.uk/

EQUAL OPPORTUNITIES COMMISSION (EOC)

Overseas House
Quay Street
Manchester M3 3HN
Tel: 0161 833 9244
Internet: http://www.eoc.org.uk/

DISABILITY RIGHTS COMMISSION

DRC Information
Freepost
MID 02 164, Stratford upon Avon
Warwickshire CV37 9BR
Tel: 0845 762 2633
Internet: http://www.drc-gb.org/

DEPARTMENT OF TRADE AND INDUSTRY (DTI)

DTI Enquiry Unit
1 Victoria Street
London SW1H 0ET
Tel: 0207 215 5000
Internet:
http://www.dti.gov.uk/er/index.htm

DEPARTMENT OF SOCIAL SECURITY (DSS)

Richmond House
79 Whitehall
London SW1A 2NS
Tel: 020 7210 6983

HEALTH AND SAFETY EXECUTIVE

St Dunstans House
201–211 Borough High Street
London SE1 1GZ
Tel: 020 7556 2100
HSE Infoline: 0870 154 5500
Internet:
http://www.hse.gov.uk/hsehome.htm

DATA PROTECTION COMMISSIONER

Office of the Information
Commissioner
Wycliffe House
Water Lane
Wilmslow
Cheshire SK9 5AF
Tel: 01625 545700
Internet:
http://www.dataprotection.gov.uk

OTHER USEFUL WEB-SITES

http://www.cipd.co.uk/
http://www.pcaw.co.uk/
http://www.redundancyhelp.co.uk/
http://www.peoplemanagement.co.uk/Index.html
http://www.ind.homeoffice.gov.uk/
http://www.successunlimited.co.uk/
http://www.harassmentlaw.co.uk/msindex.htm
http://www.wellatwork.net

Glossary

Acts of Parliament Legislation emanating from the legislature, the Houses of Parliament. Laws are recommended and laid down by the Executive (i.e. the government) and only when they are approved by the legislature (Parliament) do they become law. The judiciary (courts of law) is charged with the interpretation of law although judge-made law (common law) remains of some significance e.g. contract law.

Applicant The person who issues proceedings in the Employment Tribunal is known as the applicant. An applicant may also refer to a party who makes an interlocutory application in the civil courts

Anticipatory breach An act which indicates that one party does not intend to be bound to the contract before performance has begun or in respect of future obligations. Also known as repudiation.

Appellant The party who appeals against the decision of a civil court/Tribunal. The opposite party in appeal proceedings is known as the respondent.

Civil courts County court, High Court, Court of Appeal and House of Lords.

Claimant The party bringing an action in the civil courts, previously known as plaintiff.

Compromise Agreement An out of court settlement whereby two parties agree that one party will not pursue their full legal rights in return for compensation by way of money or benefits from the other party.

Constructive dismissal The resignation by an employee in response to a fundamental breach of contract by the employer. There is no recognised concept of 'constructive resignation'.

Contributory fault The concept of a percentage reduction of damages when the employee has by their conduct contributed to the dismissal. This is only relevant for unfair dismissal, not wrongful dismissal.

Costs order An order by the Tribunal or civil courts that one party pays the legal costs of the other.
'Costs in any event' refers to costs awarded in favour of one party regardless.
'Costs in the case' refers to costs awarded to the winning party.
'Costs reserved' refers to the award of costs being deferred to a later date.
'Costs thrown away' refers to costs awarded to a successful party when a

judgment or order in favour of the opposite party has been set aside by the court.

'Costs of and caused by' refers to costs incurred by one party as a consequence of the opposite party's conduct e.g. the defendant having to amend his defence because the claimant has amended his particulars of claim.

'Costs here and below' refers to costs awarded in favour of a party in an appeal court as well as costs incurred in lower court.

'No order as to costs' means each party bears its own costs.

COT3 Agreement An agreement between an employer and employee to settle a dispute out of court achieved with the assistance of ACAS.

Counterclaim A claim against a party who issued proceedings.

Damages Compensation for breach of contract or any other tort (civil wrong). Liquidated damages are a sum fixed by the parties in advance which is payable in the event of a breach, provided that they represent a genuine pre-estimate of loss, they are enforceable unlike penalty clauses. Unliquidated damages are a sum fixed by the court. General damages may be used to mean losses that are incapable of precise calculation (e.g. injured feelings and loss of reputation) whereas special damages refer to losses that may be quantified (e.g. loss of earnings or out of pocket expenses). Exemplary damages are awarded to punish the wrongdoer and are not awarded in breach of contract claims. Aggravated damages may be awarded where the employee's loss has been aggravated by the employer's motive or conduct.

Defendant The party who has been sued by the claimant.

Directions An order by the court that certain tasks be performed by the respective parties to a dispute prior to the actual hearing/trial including requests for further information, disclosure and inspection of documents, exchange of witness statements, appointment of experts, schedule of losses, listing for hearing.

Directors Directors may be executive or non-executive directors. Managing directors and executive directors are normally also employees of a company. A director's employment agreement (known as a service agreement) must be approved by the shareholders. Directors are normally entitled to a fee and such fees are governed by the company's articles of association.

Disclosure A process whereby a party is required to disclose evidence in his possession which is relevant to the proceedings. Disclosure may be 'standard' or 'specific'. Normally followed by inspection of those documents.

Effective date of termination The time when an employee is deemed to have been dismissed at law so that the limitation period starts to run for the purposes of commencing legal proceedings (see 2.2).

Employee An employee is someone who works under a contract of service as opposed to an independent contractor (i.e. self employed) who works under a contract for service. The courts will look at various factors to determine if someone is an employee or an independent contractor. These include the obligation to provide personal service, degree of control between the parties, integration and economic reality of the relationship. Only employees are entitled to statutory employment protection rights.

ET1 An originating application of the complainant (i.e. the employee's claim).

ET3 The respondent's case against the employee's claim (i.e. the employer's defence).

European Court of Justice The final Court of Appeal in Europe responsible for the interpretation/adjudication of European legislation when appeals in domestic courts have been exhausted.

European Court on Human Rights The European Court charged with hearing matters arising from the European Convention on Human Rights 1950 when appeals in domestic courts have been exhausted.

European legislation There are two main types of legislation emanating from Europe. Regulations are directly binding on all member states (vertical and horizontal effect). Directives are only binding on state bodies (vertical effect) until such time when it is enacted into domestic legislation after a specified time when it will have both vertical and horizontal effect. Regulations may also refer to secondary domestic legislation, e.g. statutory instruments.

Fiduciary duty A fiduciary duty arises as a result of the special relationship between two parties, e.g. solicitor and client, doctor and patient, director and shareholders. A Director owes a fiduciary duty in that he is required to act in the best interest of the Company at all times, to avoid a conflict of interest and to account for any profits made from his position.

Fundamental breach A breach of a major term or a term which goes to the root of the contract.

'Further Information' The process of requiring the other party to provide you with more information on a fact in dispute, previously known as Further and Better Particulars.

Garden leave The right to require someone not to contact clients, attend work or to work for someone else during the notice period following termination of contract. To put someone on garden leave is to quarantine the employee at home.

Injunction A Prohibitive Injunction prevents an act from being carried out whereas a Mandatory Injunction compels the performance of an act. Injunctive relief is a remedy in equity and therefore a discretionary remedy. No injunction will be granted where damages would be an adequate remedy. A temporary injunction is known as an interlocutory Injunction and normally granted on an emergency basis. If the party succeeds at the main trial, a permanent injunction called a Perpetual Injunction will be granted. Breach of an injunction is a contempt of court.

Interrogatories The process of asking the opposite party to confirm certain questions by way of written answers. This should not be used as a cross examination exercise.

Interim application/Hearing An application or hearing that is made/heard after the start of proceedings but before the main hearing/trial.

Limitation Period The time within which legal proceedings have to be presented to the Tribunal or civil courts. Some important limitation periods include: three months from the effective date of termination for unfair dismissal, three months from the date of the deduction for unlawful deduction of wages, three months from the act complained of for a discrimination claim and six months from the effective date of termination for a redundancy claim or equal pay claim. For breach of contract claims, three months from the date of the breach if brought before a tribunal or six years if adjudicated in the civil courts. Tribunals may allow applications to be made out of time in some cases. Always count three months forward less one day.

Mitigation The duty on a claimant/applicant to reduce their losses by taking reasonable steps to mitigate any damage suffered, e.g. seeking alternative employment.

Part 36 Offers A formal offer to settle a dispute before or after commencement of proceedings in the civil courts. A defendant's offer must be paid into court and kept open for 21 days. If the claimant fails to beat the defendant's payment into court at trial, the claimant is responsible for the costs of the defendant from the time when the offer was capable of being accepted until the trial.

Payment in lieu of notice Paying an employee their salary rather than requiring the employee to work out their notice period.

'Polkey principle' Where an employer has failed to follow a procedure but it can be shown that doing so would have made no difference to the decision taken by the employer, the employee's damages may be reduced to reflect the 'no difference' principle.

Pre-hearing review An interlocutory hearing to determine if a party's case has any reasonable prospect of success at the main hearing. No evidence is heard and if a party insists on pursuing a weak case, the Tribunal may require the party to pay a deposit as a condition for proceeding.

Preliminary hearing An interlocutory hearing to determine a preliminary issue e.g. whether the Tribunal has jurisdiction to hear the case or whether the employee is entitled to bring a claim. Evidence is considered in such a hearing.

Redundancy A dismissal on the basis that there is a cessation of the employer's business generally or at the place where the employee had worked or a diminution in the requirements of the employer's business generally or at the place where the employee worked. Redundancy is a fair reason for dismissal.

Re-engagement Giving the employee another job in the employer's organisation provided it is comparable to the employee's old job.

Reinstatement Giving the employee the same job back as if the employee has not been dismissed.

Respondent An employer in Tribunal proceedings. Also the opposite party to an appellant.

Statement of case This includes particulars of claim, defence, counterclaims, replies to defence and counterclaim and further information, previously known as pleadings.

Statutory Instruments Secondary or delegated legislation normally enacted pursuant to an Act of Parliament (e.g. Regulations).

Summary dismissal Dismissing someone without notice for gross misconduct.

Trust and confidence An implied term at common law that both an employer and employee will not act in a manner that will destroy the employment relationship.

Unfair Dismissal A statutory claim for dismissal under the Employment Rights Act 1996.

Without prejudice offers Informal offers for settlement made which cannot be presented as evidence in court, save as to claiming costs after the outcome of the case (see Part 36 Offers).

Witness order An order from the Tribunal requiring someone to attend the hearing failing which the witness would be in contempt and liable to a fine. In the civil courts, a person may be called to testify by way of a witness summons.

Worker A worker is a hybrid of an 'employee' and an 'independent contractor' (otherwise known as atypical employment status). Section 230(3) of the Employment Rights Act 1996 defines a worker as someone who undertakes to perform work or services personally for another party to the contract and whose relationship to the other party is not one of client or customer. A worker is legally defined to include an 'employee' and also an independent contractor whose relationship falls short of that of an employee. A worker is thus someone who is not genuinely self-employed but is economically dependent on the employer. The expansion of employment protection rights beyond 'employees' to include 'workers' is exemplified in the Sex Discrimination Act 1975, Race Relations Act 1976, Disability Discrimination Act 1995, National Minimum Wage Act 1998, Working Time Regulations 1998, Data Protection Act 1998 and Part-time Workers (Prevention of Less Favourable Treatment) Regulations 2000.

Wrongful dismissal A common law claim for breach of contract. Remedy at common law is limited to damages only. In equity, interim relief by way of injunctions may be available but specific performance is rarely granted in breach of contract claims.

Index